BLACK DEATH

J H BRENNAN

mammoth

First published in Great Britain 1995 by Mammoth
Reissued 1999 by Mammoth
an imprint of Egmont Children's Books Limited
239 Kensington High Street, London W8 6SA

ISBN 0 7497 2398 X

10 9 8 7 6 5 4 3 2 1

A CIP catalogue record for this title
is available from the British Library

Printed in Great Britain
by Cox & Wyman Ltd, Reading, Berkshire

ONE

'They died?' asked Janie, horrified.

Her father nodded.

'All of them?' She glanced past him along the village street. Sweet little thatched cottages basked in the July sunshine. Rose and honeysuckle trellises climbed their walls. A small dog trotted purposefully along the pavement. It was impossible to believe this quiet village had once been a charnel place – had been preserved *because* it was a charnel place.

Her father, John Hyde, stared thoughtfully into the middle distance. 'Every one,' he said. 'Every man, every woman, every child. There's a story that the blacksmith's son had a sweetheart in the next village who came to visit him. They wouldn't let her into Maris, of course, once the sickness started, but she used to come and stand up on the ridge. The lad would go to the edge of the village and they'd just look at one another. He'd look up at her. She'd look down at him. One day she climbed the ridge as usual, but he wasn't there. They say he was the last one to die.'

Janie could feel depression sprinkling down on her like snow. She could almost see the young lovers aching to touch one another. She could feel the agony of the girl when she climbed the ridge to find no one below. But she couldn't shake off the grisly fascination. 'How did it happen?'

'That's the awful thing,' her father said. 'It shouldn't have happened at all. The plague reached England in thirteen forty-eight, but not this far north. They think it may have come in around Weymouth. This place, Maris Caulfield, was well away from the centre of infection, but a local tailor bought a bolt of cloth that came from London. There was a flea in it.'

Janie suddenly felt sick. She knew about bubonic plague from her history class. It was caused by bacteria found in fleas that had fed on infected rats. After a flea took in blood, the plague bacteria multiplied in its stomach and eventually blocked it altogether. Then, when the flea tried to feed again, the obstruction caused the fresh blood to be vomited back into the bite, along with plague bacteria. It was all pretty gross, except that in history class it seemed sort of long ago and far away. Here, standing in a village street where it had all happened, it seemed like yesterday. She had the weird feeling that if she looked up at the ridge she would see the girl still waiting for the blacksmith's son.

With the sort of instinct that makes you pick the scab off a wound, she asked, 'What happened then?'

'The flea carried the plague.' Her father shrugged. 'The flea bit the tailor. In a couple of days he was dead ...' He shrugged again, resignedly.

2

Her father was the expert because he'd bought a booklet on the local history. All the same, she had a vague sort of half-memory of something he hadn't mentioned, although she couldn't think where she might have heard it. 'Wasn't there something nasty about the way it was handled?'

'Very nasty,' her father confirmed. 'At the time the whole district was under the jurisdiction of a sheriff – you know, like the Sheriff of Nottingham in Robin Hood. A man called FitzGerald. As soon as the tailor died, he sealed off the whole village.'

'But wasn't that a good idea?' Janie frowned. 'I mean to stop the plague spreading?'

'That was certainly FitzGerald's idea,' her father said. 'Whether it was a good idea or not depends on your viewpoint, I suppose. If you were outside the village it was a very good idea. If you were inside and wanted to escape, it must have been pretty grim.'

'What do *you* think?' Janie asked, suddenly curious.

'I don't know. After the tailor went down with the plague, his wife caught it almost at once. They both died within a day of each other. But the house was marked and nobody went near it and it was nearly two weeks before anybody else in the village showed any sign at all of the disease. All that time, FitzGerald kept them like prisoners – he had armed men on every road with orders to kill anybody from Maris on sight. Maybe if they'd been allowed to run, the tailor and his wife would have been the only victims. As it was, everybody died.'

'But at least he kept it from spreading *outside*.'

'That's the irony. It made absolutely no difference. A salt merchant carried the disease from Bristol. A couple of months after Maris Caulfield was wiped out, it was into the county anyway.'

They were walking together along the Maris Caulfield main street towards the pub where they were supposed to meet Janie's mother for lunch. Janie stopped in front of one of the pretty cottages. There was a plaque set into the wall beside the door, edged by a honeysuckle strand.

'Janet Fletcher . . .' Janie read from the plaque. 'Robert Merryweather . . . Joseph Mason . . . Barnabas Saul . . . Elizabeth Saul . . . Beth Hook . . .'

'The people who died of the plague in that house,' her father said.

'How do you know?'

He grinned. 'It says so at the bottom.'

Janie glanced down below the list of names and found he was right. 'It seems a bit . . . you know, sort of *yuck* to turn it into a tourist attraction.'

'Well, I'm not sure I'd call it a tourist attraction exactly. It's historical interest, I suppose. This was a unique event. The village wouldn't still be standing if it wasn't for the plague. Over the centuries they've renovated and rebuilt to keep it just the way it was – all because what happened was so unusual.' He tugged her sleeve to get her attention and pointed. 'See? They've preserved the old stocks on the green.'

Janie glanced over. 'So they have,' she said. 'Let's take a closer look.'

They walked across the grass. Janie stopped by the stocks, frowning. There were four holes, not the two she'd expected. She'd never seen real stocks before, but the ones in the movies only had two holes. Criminals sat on a wooden seat with their feet through them. 'What's the extra set of holes for?' she asked.

'I don't know,' her father said. 'There's a notice by you – maybe that will say.'

It was a National Trust notice which dated the stocks to the fourteenth century. There was a small drawing which explained the second pair of holes. 'They put your hands through the other holes!' exclaimed Janie, outraged. 'You went into the stocks *bent double*!' She felt sicker than she had when she'd thought about the vomiting flea. Put into the stocks like that meant you would be in agony after fifteen minutes.

'That's the way life was in the Middle Ages, I'm afraid,' her father said philosophically. 'What's the quotation – "Nasty, brutish and short"? Something like that. The stocks were mild compared to some of the other punishments, even if you *were* bent double.'

'Do I want to hear about the other punishments?' Janie asked.

Her father shook his head. 'No, I don't think you do.'

'I don't think so either.' She tossed her long black hair. 'Listen, Dad, why don't you go off and find Mum. I'd like to look around a bit more. I'll join you later at the pub.'

'What about lunch?'

'I'm not really hungry. Why don't you order me a sandwich? You and Mum can have a proper lunch and I'll have the sandwich in the car.'

'If that's what you really want . . .'

Janie watched his receding back wondering if it *was* what she really wanted. Not the sandwich, of course, but to look around the village. She'd been feeling downright strange since they arrived. She chewed her bottom lip and looked back at the stocks. They were a crude, brutal device that fascinated and repelled her at the same time. But then the whole village was like that.

She'd scarcely heard of Maris Caulfield until her mother mentioned it. The idea of taking a detour to see it hadn't been particularly appealing – she could think of better things for the last day of their holidays – but both her parents were keen. She'd been bored when they turned off the motorway, bored when they drove up the hill, bored as they passed the straggle of modern bungalows on the outskirts. Then they entered the village proper and her boredom was suddenly replaced by the weirdest feeling of . . .

Of what? A bit of her wanted to say of *déjà vu*, of strange familiarity, of having been here before. Yet she hadn't been here before, not ever, even though Maris was quite close to her home. But that wasn't all of it. Alongside the strange familiarity was another emotion, one she didn't like to look at very much. Although she'd been trying to hide it, and had hidden it, since they arrived. Maris Caulfield made her feel afraid.

TWO

There was a *wrongness* about the village and after a while she realised what it was. The houses looked too new. Not just the houses on the outskirts, which really were new, but the cottages around the common which dated back to the fourteenth century. They had fresh paint and fresh thatch and new windows set with little leaded diamond panes. They looked like cottages that had been built yesterday.

It was just renovation, of course. Exactly what you would expect since they were still lived in. There would be electric light inside, hot and cold running water, central heating. There were children playing in the trim little gardens. But while it made perfect sense, it still felt wrong.

Every cottage in the village centre had its plaque.

The names depressed her, but for some reason, Janie couldn't stop herself reading them. Even while she was walking past, she found her eye drawn casually towards the gruesome lists. *Peter Wake . . . Mary Higgs . . . Jennet Cartwright . . . Will Harper . . . Hal Dale . . . Tom Dale . . . Betsy Coke . . .* And on and on in a litany of death that stretched along the whole main street.

She found herself at the village church, a small, greystone building to the west of the common. According to a potted history on the notice board, it had been built in 1703, renovated in 1850, again in 1912 and finally again in 1952. The door was open, so she went in and immediately felt more calm. There was a leaflet on a table near the font and she glanced at it to find there had been a church building on the site since the year 1200. She noticed one church had been razed to the ground on the order of Sheriff FitzGerald in 1348 and while there was no mention of plague, the date made her suppose there must be a connection.

She came out after a while, fully intending to go straight to the pub and her parents. But she felt uneasy again as soon as she stepped into the fresh air. She stopped and tried to work out what was causing her fear. She knew exactly when it had started. The road to Maris Caulfield climbed uphill almost from the motorway, then linked with the main street in a T-junction. There were new signs at the junction directing visitors to Plague Cottages, Stocks, Museum and somewhere called Cottenham Hall. As her father swung right at this junction, the fear had gripped her like a claw in the stomach. No reason. No explanation.

The fear had stayed while they parked the car. It had stayed when her mother took her leave of them to go shopping, promising to meet up at the pub. It had stayed while she walked through the village with her father, reading the names on the plaques.

Janie had never had a nervous temperament. Yet there was something about Maris Caulfield that set her teeth on edge. She wanted to leave and she wanted to leave right away. She wanted to run to the pub, haul her parents to the car and tell her father to drive home like a bat out of hell.

Except that would be giving in to her fear.

Very deliberately, Janie walked west, away from the village square and the pub where she was supposed to meet her parents. The fear stayed with her but she ignored it. She thought she might look for the museum, or at least walk to the bottom of the ridge where the girl had climbed to watch out for her doomed sweetheart.

The old cottages round the village green gave way to modern red-brick bungalows and houses. It looked as if she'd missed the museum somehow. In fact it looked as if she was walking out of Maris Caulfield altogether. Then she saw a sign to Cottenham Hall with an arrow indicating next turn right and decided to investigate. After she'd seen the hall, she would go back to her parents.

The right turn was into a lane, far narrower than she'd expected, and a hundred metres along she began to suspect she'd gone wrong. High bramble hedges looked as though they hadn't been trimmed in years and the lane itself grew rutted and muddy. This couldn't be the road to

Cottenham Hall. She was about to turn back when the lane turned sharply.

The claw of fear in her stomach tightened abruptly. She was looking at a half-ruined, small, two-storey house which must have been at least as old as the cottages in the village centre. A portion of the roof had fallen in and every window pane was broken. To the back, a tiny orchard of twisted little trees had almost vanished beneath the undergrowth.

The building looked familiar.

It was impossible, of course. She'd never been in Maris Caulfield before, let alone walked down this creepy little lane. All the same, she felt as though she'd seen the ruin before.

There were heaps of sand and gravel near the front door, an aluminium Portacabin behind them and a JCB parked near the gateway to the orchard. But no work was going on: at least there was no sign of it.

'Hello?' Janie called uncertainly.

The high hedges with their straggle of trees left the site gloomy, despite the afternoon sunshine.

'Hello?' Janie called again.

It was strangely quiet. No birds sang in the trees, no insects hummed, there was no movement in the grass. She walked over to the Portacabin, but found it locked. On impulse she went around the back of the house. Still no one. Still no sound.

Janie licked her lips nervously. What on earth was she doing here at the back of this gloomy, creepy little dwelling? Why wasn't she walking into the pub, demanding her sandwich, encouraging her parents to get up and leave this stupid village?

One of the ground-floor windows at the back had been ripped out completely. A builder's plank was propped up against the sill and she could see scaffolding inside. Janie stared at it for a long, long time, fighting something within her. It was as if she was being drawn towards the house. Yet she was nervous of the house. Face it, she was *afraid* of the house. She stared, still drawn, still fighting. Then, almost without realising she was doing it, she started forward, walked up the plank and climbed through the hole that had once been the window.

Inside, the floor was mainly rubble, crisscrossed by more planks. A portion of wall had been removed and the ceiling above it was now supported by two large builder's jacks. A small fireplace and mantel leaned together in a corner of the room while a gaping hole opposite showed where they had been taken out. A wooden door, half hanging from one hinge, led into a dingy little passage-way.

'Is anybody here?' Janie called. She wondered how she was going to explain what she was doing if anybody *was* there. She looked around. She was having difficulty explaining it even to herself.

There was no sound inside the building.

Janie clambered over the planks, edged her way through the network of scaffolding and pushed past the hanging door into the narrow passage. An errant nail caught the pocket of her jeans and ripped. *Damn!* They were brand-new, bought specially for the holiday. Janie examined the damage in the gloom, decided there was nothing she could do until later and pressed on.

The passage led to a small door secured by a padlock, and a flight of narrow stairs. She looked up the stairs for a moment, wondering if they were safe, then started to climb. Her footsteps echoed on the wooden treads.

Although she was not particularly tall, she had to stoop in the corridor above. Three rooms opened off it, each of them up a single step, none of them with a door. A scrap of tattered curtain hung over the entrance to one of the rooms. Cement dust caught in her throat and rubble crunched underfoot.

The two rooms she could see were empty. One of them had what looked to be a new wooden floor. What was she *doing* here? She was certainly trespassing and if anybody came back now she would not have even a shred of an excuse. What's more, the house frightened her. She was creeping through it for some reason she couldn't understand and she was very much afraid. The claw in her stomach was tighter than at any time since she'd entered this ghastly village.

It was stupid. She would turn and go back down the stairs and climb out through the window and *leave*. She would run up the narrow little lane and run back into the village and run down to the pub and tell her parents she was feeling ill so they'd—

She walked to the third room and pulled back the curtain.

The room had a low, sloping ceiling with dark, narrow beams. There were rushes on the floor (*rushes?*) and a straw pallet on a rough wooden frame pushed up against one wall. Beside it was a dark oakwood chest, crudely made. There were rushlights (*rushlights?*) burning in wall holders. A woman in a long dress and apron was standing by the window.

Janie blinked. The room was empty. The claw in her stomach turned to iron. She felt the pressure in her chest that was the first sign of an asthma attack and remembered with a feeling of near panic that she'd left her inhaler in the car. She fell back a step, unable to believe what she'd seen, unable to believe what she was seeing. The room was definitely empty, one wall part replastered. There was no carpet of rushes, no oak chest, no crude bed, no woman.

But she'd *seen* the woman!

Janie turned and stumbled down the corridor, her chest heaving. The asthma was building with its old familiar fury. She took the stairs as fast as she dared and actually ran along the narrow passage. She felt more frightened now than she had ever been in her life. The dust in the passage billowed up to fill her lungs and when she coughed, her head began to spin. She knew she had to get outside or she was in danger of blacking out. She pushed into what should have been the room with the scaffolding and found herself in a kitchen. From somewhere to her right there were heavy footfalls and a brief burst of laughter.

She was no longer in a kitchen, but in some dark, airless space which pressed in on her like some soft, dank, suffocating vice. She had to get out! From the darkness a hand reached out to stroke her hair. Janie screamed, except that the scream emerged as a chest-heaving gasp. She fell against a wall, found a door and opened it.

Dust-free air flooded her lungs. She clung to the doorpost, head down, gasping and panting. If she could manage to relax, she might control the asthma long enough to get back to the car and her inhaler. She fought with her heaving lungs. She could not manage a full breath, nor even a half-breath. All the same, her head was clearing a little.

She was outside the house. She must have left by the front door. *Drop your shoulders! Think calm!* It was nearly impossible to think calm while gasping for air. All the same, she was out of the house. Her mind presented her with a memory of the bedroom upstairs, of the woman by the window, turning, turning to face her. *Calm! Calm!* Her heart was pounding.

She knew she had to get away from the house. There was no way she could achieve a state of calm while standing in its shadow. She straightened. It was only a matter of willpower.

Her eye caught the plaque by the door. It must have been the first thing the renovators had put up. Janie decided she loathed Maris Caulfield with its little lists of ancient death. *Rob Willis,* she read, *Rebecca Willis, Alan Hyde, Jayne Hyde . . .*

She could not take her eyes off the name. *Jayne Hyde. Jayne Hyde. Jayne Hyde.* It swam from the plaque and danced around her mockingly. *Jayne Hyde.* The same name as her own.

THREE

Her father glanced up. 'Janie, what on earth's the matter?'

But her mother was already on her feet. 'She's having an asthma attack.' She put her arm around Janie's shoulders. 'Where's your inhaler, darling?'

The pub was in the middle of its lunch-time rush and Janie was aware people were turning to look at her, but she was well past caring. 'Car!' she managed to gasp out.

'John, have you got the car keys?' her mother asked firmly.

'It's all right, I'll come with you.' He took her arm and together her parents herded her out of the pub. Neither of them said another word until they reached the car. Janie reached in and grabbed her inhaler gratefully from the glove compartment. She popped the nozzle in her mouth and pressed the plunger. The fine spray eased the pressure on her chest at once and she gulped in deep draughts of air. The familiar medicinal taste remained in her mouth.

'All right now, darling?' her father asked quietly.

Janie nodded. She gave a weak smile. 'Sorry for the fuss.'

'For heaven's sake don't apologise!' her mother exclaimed.

'Bit embarrassing in a crowded pub,' Janie grinned sheepishly.

Her father shrugged. 'You couldn't help it. Are you really all right now?'

'Much better,' Janie said truthfully. 'My own silly fault for leaving the inhaler in the car.'

'What happened?' her mother asked.

Janie tried to shrug it off. She had no intention of telling them anything about her experiences at the house. They were far too weird for comfort. 'Oh, you know,' she said vaguely. 'It always hits at the stupidest times. It wouldn't have developed at all if I hadn't forgotten my inhaler.'

Her father would have bought it, but her mother wasn't so easily put off. 'You've torn your jeans,' she said.

Janie smiled weakly. 'Yes, well—'

'Your shirt's filthy and you've got dust in your hair – you look nearly as grey as I am.'

'Look, Mum—' Janie began. She hadn't the slightest idea what she was going to say, but fortunately her father came to the rescue.

'Maybe we can talk about this later,' he said. 'She looks as though she could do with getting home: hot bath and a bit of an early night, eh?'

Janie smiled at him gratefully. 'I *do* feel a bit ropy still, Dad.'

Her mother looked suspicious, but her father was already sliding behind the wheel of the car.

Janie climbed into the back and quickly closed her eyes to stop any more awkward questions. They were less than an hour from home and by pretending to be asleep, she could buy herself time to think. Now the immediate crisis of the asthma was over, she had to figure out what had happened. And not just to keep her mother quiet: she needed to know what had happened for herself.

A picture of the half-ruined, part-renovated house arose on the backs of her eyelids. There was nothing at all familiar about it, yet it felt familiar. There was no reason why she should have hung around for a moment after discovering she'd missed the turn for Cottenham Hall, yet she'd hung around. There was certainly no reason why she should have gone into the house, yet she'd gone in.

Why?

She could imagine her mother asking the question, but she had no answer, not for her mother, not for herself.

Why did Maris Caulfield make her feel afraid? She didn't know the answer to that one either, but she was definitely feeling better now the car was carrying her out of the plague village. She opened her eyes a slit to discover they were now on the hill road back to the motorway and felt a surge of relief that left her almost breathless again. It was ridiculous to feel like this. It was even more ridiculous not to know why.

She closed her eyes again. The whole thing was crazy, but none of it so crazy as what she'd seen in the bedroom of the house. Had the woman been a ghost?

Maybe she'd just imagined it.

Somehow Janie couldn't believe she'd just imagined it.

The July sun brought a soothing heat into the car and Janie found her mind drifting to the steady whirr of the engine. Her mother began to talk softly to her father and while Janie suspected the conversation might be about her, the words blurred into a background hum. What had happened? she asked herself again. What had happened in the weird little house?

Janie looked down at her feet and her feet were brown and bare. She looked down at her hands and they were not her own hands. They were a woman's hands, square and strong with rough skin on the palms. There was a thin wedding ring on her left third finger.

She was wearing an apron over a long coarse dress over heavy petticoats and her bottom, underneath the skirt, was bare. Although she'd never gone without pants in her life, she felt no surprise. The dress, a dun brown, felt familiar.

A hoarse voice on her left whispered, 'And I looked, and behold a pale horse: and his name that sat on him was Death, and Hell followed with him.'

Janie swung round, but there was no one there. She was standing on a winding path that turned and twisted through a barren countryside. Beside her, a skull and three rib-bones protruded from a shallow heap of loam. For some reason she thought about the house and the heaps of sand and gravel the builders had left.

She began to walk along the winding track. She could feel sharp pebbles beneath her bare feet, but they did not hurt. Her chest felt a little tight from the residue of her asthma, but that was all right because she had her inhaler in her apron pocket.

The path began to climb, like the road to Maris Caulfield, and she saw silhouetted on the horizon a tall rider on a pale horse. He turned his head to stare at her, then wheeled the horse around and disappeared. Janie stood absolutely still for a very long time, knowing she must never draw too close to the rider on the pale horse.

She left the path and began to walk across the barren land. Everywhere she walked, skulls and bones protruded from the earth as if the whole world had become a giant graveyard.

A church spire appeared on the horizon and Janie walked towards it. There was safety in the church. She had ceased to feel afraid in Maris church. If she hurried she could reach it before the Sheriff burned it down. But as she hurried, the church spire receded.

Somewhere there was the sound of a bell, but not a church bell. She knew now she would never reach the safety of the church. The bell sounded like a handbell, clanging so mournfully she felt a tear escape from one eye. She dabbed it away as a hunchback limped into view wheeling a wooden barrow.

He was the ugliest creature she had ever seen. His lower lip hung wetly, his eyes were rheumy and bloodshot, his face a mass of warts. He smiled when he saw her, showing broken teeth. 'You saw the pale horse,' he said in a rasping voice.

'It was you who spoke to me,' said Janie. Despite his ugliness, she did not feel afraid.

He was dressed in the filthiest of rags. Now one hand emerged from the rags and reached towards her, beckoning. 'See,' he said, 'see what's in my cart!' There was something in his cart covered with sacking.

Fear welled up in Janie's stomach.

'Come see,' whispered the hunchback enticingly.

Janie knew she must not see what was in the hunchback's cart.

The hunchback tweaked the edge of the sacking. 'Look, Missy, look what's in my cart.'

Janie turned to run, but the hunchback was now behind her. He grinned broadly. She turned back. He was in front of her again. There were lights dancing in his bloodshot eyes. His bony finger beckoned.

One foot moved before the other. Janie slowly walked towards the cart.

'That's it,' said the hunchback. 'That's a *good* girl.' He reached over again and gripped the edge of the sacking.

She must not look at what was in the cart. She must not know what was in the cart.

The hunchback drew her with his mind. She

could not stop herself moving forward. The blossom of fear was a hideous flower that commanded her whole soul. She must not see the horror in the cart.

As she walked towards the hunchback, Janie began to scream.

'Darling, what's the matter?'

She sat up, panting, her heart still racing. She was in the car, her mother's hand on her shoulder, shaking her. Janie looked around, disoriented. Eventually she said, 'A dream. Just a bad dream.'

She tugged a handkerchief from the torn pocket of her jeans and wiped a trickle of sweat from her forehead.

FOUR

Toby walked into the coffee shop, kissed her cheek and sat down. 'You look terrible,' he said.

'Thanks,' Janie said coolly. All the same, she felt better for being with him again. He was a stocky boy who never knew how to dress and he was a couple of centimetres shorter than she was, but she'd still turned down the Games Captain so she could go out with him.

Toby looked round and started to wave wildly for the waitress. 'Rotten holiday?' he asked.

'Bad dreams,' Janie said. She was wondering how much she should tell him, but bad dreams seemed safe enough.

The waitress came over, chewing a stub of pencil. 'Hi, Toby,' she said. 'Cappuccino, one sugar?'

'Right,' said Toby. 'Listen, Stella, I need a burger first; and chips. Fat burger with cheese and no onions.' He turned to Janie. 'You don't mind, do you – I haven't eaten all day.'

'No, of course not.'

'I eat fast – we'll still be in time for the main feature. You want another one of those things?'

Janie shook her head. She'd been spooning an

Italian ice-cream with a runny toffee sauce. It was real comfort food and God knew she needed comfort, but too many of them put on weight.

Stella wrote on her pad. 'Cheeseburger and fries, hold the onions, cappuccino, one sugar,' she said cheerfully. She tapped Toby on the head with her pencil. 'Coming up!'

Toby turned to Janie. 'How come you're having bad dreams? Did you miss me that much?'

'No,' Janie said. She smiled. 'Well, I did, actually. The holiday was a bit of a bore. You know how it is when you have to go with parents.'

'Tell me about it!' Toby groaned. 'You tramp over every ruin in sight and then they're too tired to go to the disco.'

Janie's smile broadened, then faded. 'You ever hear of Maris Caulfield?'

'Sure,' Toby said. 'It's the plague village.'

'Ever been there?'

'No way!' He shuddered. 'I'm a paid-up hypochondriac. Take me to a place like that and the rash would start inside five minutes. That's not where you stayed, was it?'

'No, but we paid a visit on the way home – Mum wanted to see it.' Janie stopped.

'And . . .?' Tony asked, leaning forward encouragingly.

She decided to tell him. Toby was the sort of boy you could talk to about anything. He didn't tease. He didn't jeer. He didn't mock. He didn't pass on secrets. He was probably the best listener she'd ever known. That was why she was sitting here with him now, not stretched out on a back seat fumbling with some hunk of a jock like the Games Captain.

'And I saw a ghost,' she said bleakly.

Stella bustled back with a tray and unloaded Toby's cheeseburger, chips and cappuccino. He paid her, then turned back to Janie. 'You're having me on, right?' He studied her expression. 'You're not having me on.'

'No, I'm not,' Janie said. 'At least, I don't think so. I'm not sure what it was.'

There was ketchup in a plastic tomato in the middle of the table and Toby squeezed a pool of it on to the side of his plate. He forked a chip, dipped it and ate it. 'Better you tell me everyzing, mein dear,' he said in a Viennese accent.

'I didn't like the place,' Janie said.

'Maris?' He ate another chip.

She nodded. 'It gave me the creeps. They have these plaques all over with the names of the people who died in the plague. I mean, I know it doesn't sound much, but when you're *there* . . .'

'Yes, it's sort of gross,' Toby agreed.

'Anyway, that wasn't it. I was looking around – Mum and Dad were at the pub – and I came on this old house. Bit of a ruin somebody was fixing up. I went in and—'

'You went in?'

Janie nodded. 'Yes.'

'Why?' Toby asked.

That was another thing about him. He had a talent for asking pertinent questions. 'I don't know why,' she said. 'I just did.'

'OK.' Toby started on his cheeseburger.

'The odd thing was, there was a plaque on this house and one of the people who died had the same name as me.' She shrugged. 'Anyway, there was a room upstairs and when I looked in I saw the ghost. The whole room was sort of, like, fourteenth century and there was a woman in there in old-fashioned gear. Then next thing, it was an ordinary room again, empty.'

'What was the rest of the house like?' Toby asked.

'Empty,' Janie said. 'They had workmen in. I mean, there wasn't anybody there while I was there, but there was, you know, scaffolding and stuff all over the place.'

'So what happened when the ghost disappeared?'

'I had an asthma attack,' Janie told him.

Toby chewed on his burger. 'Wow,' he said thoughtfully, 'that was a real bummer.'

'That's not really the problem,' Janie said.

'What's really the problem then?'

'Afterwards, in the car on the way back home, I had this dream about a hunchback. It was terrifying and I don't know why. He tried to show me something he had in a wooden cart. I know that doesn't sound terrifying, but it was.'

'Dreams are funny that way,' Toby agreed.

'Anyway, the thing is, I keep having this dream. I've had it every night since. Every night, Toby – that's what? We came back on Sunday and I had it Sunday night as well as in the car and it's Friday now so I've had it Sunday, Monday, Tuesday, Wednesday, Thursday – five nights. Every night I get closer to seeing what's in the cart and it's scarier and scarier. I wake up in a sweat and I can't get back to sleep and I'm afraid of going to bed now and I'm exhausted all the time. It's no wonder I look terrible!' To her embarrassment, she began to cry uncontrollably.

Toby reached out and took her hand. 'Hey, it's going to be all right!'

She looked up at him, desperate for comfort and found it, somehow, in the way he looked. 'Is it?'

Toby nodded. 'It is. You didn't tell anybody about this, right?'

'No.'

'I mean, not your parents or anybody? Not about the ghost or the nightmare?'

'No, I – I mean, they're not into that sort of thing. Can you imagine my father believing in a *ghost*? He's an architect, for heaven's sake! I was afraid they'd laugh.'

'That's what I thought,' Toby said. 'And that's where you went wrong.'

Janie wiped the remainder of her tears with her handkerchief. 'I did?'

'Sure you did. Look at the pyschology. Maris Caulfield gives you the creeps. It's got notices about dead people all over the place. It's no wonder you saw a ghost.'

'Do you think it was a real ghost?' Janie asked.

Toby shrugged. 'I don't know. But whether it was a real ghost or not, that isn't your problem.

The ghost isn't hassling you – it's the nightmare that's hassling you.'

'Yes, that's true.'

'I expect the nightmare came from Maris Caulfield as well. You're a sensitive girl and the place upset you. But the thing about nightmares is, they're stuff that's trying to come up from the unconscious – in this case, the creepy feelings you had about Maris Caulfield. As long as you keep pushing that stuff down, it keeps bobbing up again like a cork. The trick to getting rid of a nightmare is to *let it out*.' He dropped briefly into his Michael Caine imitation and said, 'Not many people know that.' He became serious again. 'But it's true. The best way to stop having a nightmare about something is to think about it very consciously just before you go to sleep. That way it doesn't have to push up from the unconscious.'

'So all I have to do is think about the hunchback and I won't dream about him again?'

'You probably won't even have to do that,' Toby predicted. 'I'm prepared to bet you a five-pound note – which is all I have in the world after tonight – I'm prepared to bet a fiver that now you've talked about it, now you've *let it out*, you won't have that nightmare again. You'll sleep like a baby.'

He had such an air of certainty about him that Janie felt flooded with relief. 'You really think so?'

'I've just bet on it,' said Toby. He finished the last of his burger, took a sip of cappuccino and pushed back his chair. 'Come on, or we'll miss the start of the movie.'

'Where are we going?' Janie asked.

'Well,' said Toby, 'I was planning to take you to the Classic, but it'll have to be the Odeon now.'

'Why's that?'

He took her arm. 'The Classic's showing a rerun of *The Hunchback of Notre Dame*,' he grinned.

FIVE

Toby lost his bet just two nights later. The real horror was that Janie knew she was dreaming, but couldn't wake up.

The nightmare started like all the others with the long winding path and the voice whispering, *And I looked, and behold a pale horse . . .* But this time, when she looked, Janie did not see the tall rider, but rather the hunchback and his cart no more than three metres from her.

She knew she was dreaming at once, but it did her no good. 'No!' she screamed at the hunchback. 'Get away from me!'

'But you must see what I have in my cart,' the hunchback said, grinning and drooling. He lurched towards her.

Unable to wake up, Janie fled. Her feet flew over the rough ground and she ran with great ease, but the hunchback caught up with her. A powerful hand gripped her arm and she could smell his body odour like old, rank cheese. She struggled wildly, but he dragged her back towards the cart. As they approached it, she could see the sacking begin to slip away, and redoubled her struggles.

'Let me go! Let me go!'

They had reached the cart now. His hand went out towards the sacking. 'See?' he said. 'See what I have in my cart?'

But she woke then, sweating, terrified and close to tears because the nightmare she believed gone – the nightmare Toby told her was over – had now returned. For a long moment she lay in the darkness praying the fear wouldn't trigger her asthma. What was happening to her? Toby said it was just old fears pushing up from her unconscious, but she'd talked about it to him and she'd even deliberately thought about the hunchback before coming to bed and the nightmare *still* happened.

It happened again the next night. And the next. That third night was the worst. The hunchback had dragged her all the way over to the cart and was removing the sacking when she awoke. Her pyjamas and sheets were so drenched with sweat it looked as if she'd wet the bed. Even in her terror she was so concerned about what her mother might say that she changed the sheets, changed her pyjamas for a night-shirt and dropped the sodden items in the wash downstairs. Her whole instinct urged her to wash them there and then, but she resisted. The sound of the machine was bound to wake her parents and they'd want to know what on earth she was doing in the middle of the night. All the same, she got up early next morning and pushed a load of washing (with sheets and pyjamas) through. Her mother thanked her for it later.

Getting up early was no problem because she could hardly sleep anyway. She'd go to bed and lie awake worrying about the nightmare, then drift into sleep and the dream. Then she'd wake, gasping and sweating, and lie awake for the rest of the night.

The nightmare came again on the fourth night which was the Thursday. Next day she was feeling so wretched she called Toby and cancelled their regular Friday-night date without explaining why. She also resisted his suggestion they go out Saturday or meet Sunday afternoon. He sounded disappointed and she knew he must be confused, but she was too tired to explain.

The hunchback was waiting for her again that Friday night and on the Saturday after an early night, a video of *The Lion King* (if Disney couldn't take your mind off horror, what could?) and a glass of malted milk. He took the night off on Sunday, but that didn't do much good because Janie hung in there for hours after she'd gone to bed, waiting for him right up to the moment she fell into an exhausted, fitful dreamless sleep.

Exhaustion had become a way of life with her. Only her parents' busy schedules – and a little judicious make-up – prevented their noticing something was amiss. Toby would know something was wrong at once, of course, but she wasn't due to see him until next Friday and she could always put him off again. She was sorry now she'd confided in him in the first place.

On Monday the nightmare *did* trigger an asthma attack. She cut it short with the inhaler, which was on her bedside table, but the very fact it happened convinced her things were really getting out of hand. She still didn't know what to do. There was a fear in her now that was greater than her fear of the hunchback. It was a fear she wanted to look at even less than she wanted to look into his cart. But this fear was now so great it was forcing her to look, forcing her to acknowledge its reality. Exhausted, haunted, nightmare-ridden, Janie Hyde was beginning to fear she was losing her mind.

On Tuesday afternoon, the hallucinations started.

SIX

Janie was a day pupil at Haresden High School, an ugly, interesting mix of Victorian buildings and modern, Scandinavian-style extensions set in what had once been a small country estate, but was now a shrinking oasis of greenery surrounded by housing estates.

There was roast beef and plastic gravy for lunch on Tuesday, served with Yorkshire pud so stodgy that even in her exhaustion Janie wondered ruefully if it might be a plot to keep pupils under control. She walked to physics class to the accompaniment of Helen Craig's incessant chatter.

'Well, do you?' Helen asked insistently.

'Do I what?' asked Janie, who hadn't been listening.

Helen sighed dramatically. 'Do you know your sun sign?'

'Yes, of course,' said Janie. 'It's Cancer.'

'Well, there you are then!' Helen exclaimed bewilderingly. As an afterthought she added, 'Did you know some astrologers don't call it Cancer any more because it sounds too much like you'd just caught the Big C? They tell you you're a Moonchild instead.'

'Really?' Janie said politely.

She sat in physics class while Mr Howarth droned on about neutrinos, her stomach leaden, vaguely wondering if finding you had the Big C could be any worse than thinking you were losing your mind. She glanced out the window.

'Come on, Jayne,' Alan said, wheedling and grinning. 'We be allowed to do it any time we want, now we be married.'

She slapped his hand away. 'You behave yourself, Alan Hyde. Married or no, I got chickens to feed.'

'Leave the fool chickens,' Alan told her crossly. He was a big, florid red-haired man who'd become very demanding since they were wed. Not that Jayne minded – the priest had told her it was a wife's duty, after all – but her parents were living in the house and they'd know what was happening if she allowed him to drag her off upstairs.

'Leave them, is it?' she asked sharply. 'And who'll be feeding them then? Not you, Alan Hyde, I'll be bound.' She pushed past him and made off briskly across the yard, hoping he wouldn't follow. Sometimes when the urge was on him he grew persistent and then they fought. She hated fights.

He didn't follow, but turned away sulkily and walked off in the direction of the Big House where he sometimes helped the stable lads. She felt a brief pang of guilt. He wasn't a bad man. He worked hard, drank little and had never hit her, not even now they'd married. If he could just get it into his head that things had their proper time and place. The trouble was, he was a little simple. But then she'd known that before she married him. Her mother even thought it was a good thing. A simple man was easier to control – at least in some ways.

The hens heard her approach and ran forward enthusiastically, but she was in no hurry to feed them now he had gone. She walked over to the gate and leaned on it, staring out across the fields, her eye drawn to the cart track that led to the village. She was not sorry she'd married Alan, however difficult he might be at times. He'd made no objection to her parents living with them, even though it was his house by right now. He even humoured her father when he insisted he knew the best way to run the little farm. *Aye, Rob, that could be so*, she'd heard him answer half a dozen times a day. Even when her father criticised him openly (which he should never have done) it was still the same placid answer. *Aye, Rob, that could be so.*

A hen pecked her ankle sharply and she looked down to find herself surrounded by the scrawny birds. She took a handful of grain from her apron and threw it far from her so that they scattered. She'd managed to build up quite a flock, thanks to the activities of that strutting little rooster. She grinned to herself. Maybe that was where Alan got his ideas.

She turned back to the gate and saw there was someone on the cart track now, too far to make out his features, but the donkey he rode meant it must be Father Maris. He would be on his way to the Big House – Squire Burston was a pious man who paid to have Mass said in the family chapel every second day – but he might stop off for a word or two if he wasn't running late. Jayne hoped he would. She liked Father Maris. He was ill-educated and dull, like most of the priests, but at least he didn't try to put his hand up your skirt during Confession and his Penances were light. In the village, Jennet Cartwright said he was a truly holy man, perhaps even saintly. Jayne was not so sure, but she liked to ask his blessing just the same. If he really *was* a saint, then the blessings would make sure she had a place in Heaven.

She turned and tossed more grain to keep the hens away, then opened the gate and slipped outside. If she walked to meet Father Maris, then she could walk back with him even if he was late. Just being with a saint (if he *was* a saint) would surely mean an increase in your merit. All helped. The Devil was abroad, day and night. There was sickness in London. A woman couldn't be too careful, not even a goodwife who never missed Mass of a Sunday.

He was riding head bowed, as if dozing, but some sixth sense must have alerted him, for he looked up at her approach and smiled a welcome. He was an ugly little man with yellowing eyes and dirty fingernails, but she often thought he had a very pleasing voice – and one that seemed too large for that small body.

'Goodwife Hyde,' he said in his large voice.

'Father Maris.' Jayne curtsied politely.

'I'm sorry?' said Mr Howarth, frowning.

Janie stared at him, blinking away her bewilderment.

'Who's Father Maris?' Howarth asked.

Janie shook her head. 'I don't know.' Around her, the class began to titter.

SEVEN

It happened again on Wednesday while she was on the school bus back home. She was staring out of the window, head heavy from lack of sleep and sank into a doze. The doze might have slipped into a dream, but this was no dream.

She walked across grass towards the little stone-built church. Her husband Alan was by her side, complaining. Unusually for him, he had drunk too much ale the night before and resented having to get out of his bed this morning.

'Don't see why we has to be at Mass *every* Sunday,' he grumbled. 'Lots of folk miss it now and then, for sickness and such.'

'Lots of folks die and go straight to Hell,' she told him bluntly. 'Which is what you'll do if you miss your Mass for no better reason than a bellyful of ale.'

'So *you* say,' he muttered sulkily. His bottom lip pouted and he examined his feet as he walked. In many ways he was like a child and, as she often did, she treated him like a child now.

She reached out and took his hand, a large, rough hand that swallowed hers. 'God wants us to come to Mass,' she told him gently, 'because in the Mass the Lord Jesus takes away our sins and keeps us safe. You knows that, don't you?'

His head came up as he said, 'Oh aye.' But his tone showed he wasn't altogether mollified.

She tried another tack, her voice still coaxing and gentle, 'And you knows God punishes the sinners, don't you, Alan?'

'Oh aye.'

'He's punishing the godless in London right this minute,' she said with the faintest hint of grim satisfaction. It was true enough. According to Father Maris and Squire Burston both, the Black Death was raging in London now, seeking out sinners in the stews and the bawdy houses, striking down the unrighteous just as it had done in foreign parts. She shivered a little at the thought. God's wrath had fallen mightily on the filthy foreigners. She had heard it all from the Squire when he warned his tenantry about the need for purity as the only sure form of protection.

Nobody quite knew where the sickness started – some said India, some Cathay – but just two years ago it had reached the Italian trading stations in the Crimea. Within months the death toll had climbed to eighty-five thousand. Local Tartars – mindless pagans that they were – decided it was all the fault of decent Christian merchants and mounted an attack on a Genoese trading station in the city of Tana. The merchants fled to Feodosia. Pursuing Tartars settled down outside the city walls to lay siege. But before they could do much, God saw that the plague caught up with them. In days their numbers were decimated.

The Tartars called off the siege, but with deep Satanic cunning they had seen that those who came close to plague victims often fell ill themselves. So they loaded the pus-filled bodies of their dead colleagues into giant catapults and flung them over the city walls.

The Genoese dumped the corpses into the sea, but the damage was already done. As plague spread through Feodosia, its citizens quickly realised the few who were likely to survive could never defend against a renewed Tartar attack. There was a mass panic-stricken exodus by sea.

These ships, along with trading galleys from infected Eastern ports, put in at Genoa, at Venice, at Messina, but by then their crews were dying at their oars. When the port authorities saw the cargoes of corpses, they sent the ships packing. But as in Feodosia, action came a little too late. While the authorities made their inspections, the plague landed. Banished from their docks, the galleys simply sought other ports, thus spreading the disease even further. By the following year, the plague – now known as the 'Blue Sickness' and the 'Black Death' – was raging throughout Sicily. Three months later, it had taken a firm hold on the Italian mainland.

Towards the end of January this year, the dreadful pattern repeated. A plague-ridden galley, banished from Italy, put in at Marseilles. Port authorities came on board to inspect and left infected. The ship was chased off and carried its cargo of death to Spain.

God sent the disease eastwards as well. Dalmatia was plague-ridden. Dubrovnik went under. Wolves poured in from the neighbouring forests to attack the few survivors. Piles of corpses rotted in the streets – there was no one left to bury them.

None of this was really surprising, Squire Burston said. Everyone knew the French and the Italians and the Russians had turned their faces from God years before. But now the horror had reached England and that was a different story. Some said it had come in at Bristol, some at Southampton, but wherever it came in, it had really taken hold in London and there was an important lesson to be learned from that. All knew the Londoners were nearly as godless as the French. It was obvious God had decided He was not to be mocked any longer. What was happening in London was a sign to the rest of the country. *Mend your ways*, Squire Burston said, *else the Black Death could take even you!*

'So we must go to Mass so God won't punish us as well?' said Alan brightly.

She squeezed his hand. 'That's it exactly, Alan! Now you understand.'

The Mass was beautiful as always. The flickering candles in the tiny, gloomy little church made Jayne feel this must be how Heaven looked at night: bright, dancing lights and the sweet, sacred smell of incense. When Father Maris raised the chalice, she felt tears of gratitude trickle down her cheeks. She had no fear of the Blue Sickness. Gentle Jesus would protect her and those she held dear.

When the Mass was over, she left the church feeling lightened, as if God Himself had reached down and taken away her sins. Even Alan's mood had changed, for he smiled and saluted his cronies, including, she suspected, one or two who'd been with him the night before, drinking ale. She felt a sudden warmth in her heart towards him. There was no real harm in her big, red-headed, simple husband, no real harm at all.

'Good morrow, Jayne,' a soft voice said on her left.

She turned to find Elizabeth Saul, the tailor's wife, at her elbow. 'Good morrow, Bess,' she said, smiling. Although Goodwife Saul was near ten years older than she was, they had become friends on account of an arrangement that gave eggs for sewing. She looked around. 'Your Barnabas not with you?'

Bess Saul shook her head. 'Nay, his head and gut was paining so bad I could not persuade him out of bed this morning.'

'Perchance he was taking ale last night with my Alan,' Jayne said, glancing with mock severity at her husband.

But Alan shook his head. 'Nay,' he said soberly, 'Mr Saul bain't never drunk with me, Jayne.' He blinked his large eyes and looked from one woman to the other. 'Tailor must be sickening for something,' he said.

She felt a sharp elbow in her ribs and looked

round into the face of Helen Craig. 'This is your *stop*!' hissed Helen.

Janie glanced through the window. 'Yipes!' She grabbed her books and bustled down the aisle. 'Thanks, Helen!' she called over her shoulder and jumped from the bus just as it was starting to pull away from the stop.

She stood on the empty pavement watching the receding vehicle. Helen waved to her from a window, but Janie did not wave back. The whole vision of the church and the conversation flooded through her. She wanted to believe she had been dreaming, but she knew it was no dream. She could smell the incense, hear the voice of Goodwife Saul. It had none of the shifting, unreal quality of a dream, any more than it had had in physics class the day before. It felt as real and solid as her morning shower.

She began to walk towards her home, feeling the heaviness of exhaustion in every step. What was happening to her? Her nights were tormented by the hunchback and now her days had started to be haunted by these . . . these . . .

These what? Visions? Waking dreams? They were so real. It felt as if she had somehow walked out of her world, walked out of the here and now, walked into some weird *elsewhere*. When she returned, the memory was as vivid as if she'd actually been living somewhere else. If it wasn't a dream or a vision, there was only one more thing it could be – an hallucination. And an hallucination confirmed what she'd already started to suspect: her mind was cracking.

She needed to talk to somebody. But who? Toby was easy to talk to, but what could he do? He was three years older than she was, holding down his first job as a trainee clerk in an export company. What would he know about mental illness? He might sympathise, but what could he do? (And a part of her was afraid that while he might sympathise, he might also *walk*. There weren't many boys who wanted to go out with a girl heading helter-skelter for the funny farm. Janie had troubles enough just now. She didn't want to add losing Toby to the list.)

She didn't want to tell her parents either. She didn't know what her father would do – sometimes she didn't think she really knew her father at all – but her mother would freak. And a freak-out in these circumstances was more than Janie could face. Her mother was Action Woman. She listened minimally, then had to *do* something. Janie shuddered to think what might happen with her mother pushing the buttons.

But if not Toby and if not her parents, then who? Janie let herself into the empty house, flung herself down on the living-room sofa and fell immediately asleep. For once the hunchback did not come.

EIGHT

She felt better when she woke. She swung her feet off the couch, knuckled the sleep from her eyes, then saw her father sitting in the chair opposite. He was staring at her intently.

'Ready to talk about it?' he asked soberly.

Janie blinked. 'About what, Dad?'

Her father sighed. 'Come on, Janie, do you think I'm blind or stupid? You look like death, you've been creeping round the house in the middle of the night, you yawn through every meal, it's almost impossible to get two words out of you. What's the problem? Are you pregnant?'

She was so surprised she laughed out loud. The expression on his face made her laugh even more. She realised it was the first time she'd really laughed since they visited Maris Caulfield. She slid from the couch, knelt in front of him and took his hand with a sudden immense fondness. 'No, Dad, I'm not pregnant – not even slightly.'

He looked relieved, but still said, 'What is it then?'

Janie's smile faded. 'I'm not sure it isn't worse than pregnant.'

'At your age, *nothing's* worse than pregnant,' her father said. 'Believe me.'

Janie glanced around. 'Is Mum home?'

'Not yet. I reckon you have maybe three-quarters of an hour to tell me.' He grinned conspiratorially.

'And you won't tell her?'

'Not if you don't want me to.'

'I don't,' said Janie with feeling. 'At least not yet.' She hesitated, took a deep breath and told him everything.

He listened without interrupting and without a flicker of expression. When she had finished, he said, 'You need help.'

'I need locking up,' Janie told him dourly.

He grinned, pouting. 'Maybe soon, but not yet.' The grin vanished. 'Would you go to a doctor if I set it up for you?'

He was so relaxed she confronted her fear. 'Dad, I'm not sure an ordinary doctor is going to hack it.'

'I know what you mean, but I'm not sure I agree.'

'Dad, I'm *hallucinating*!'

He shrugged. 'That's a very harsh way of putting it.'

'How would *you* put it?'

'Well,' he said seriously, 'I wouldn't underestimate the effect of lack of sleep. You remember Billy Hyland?'

She nodded. Mr Hyland was an American friend of her father's. He'd visited them briefly last year.

'Billy served in Vietnam – did you know that? He told me one time he got separated from his platoon and spent five days in the jungle. He was so scared of the Viet Cong he hardly slept a wink. By the time he got back to base, he was hallucinating. He told me he used to see giant spiders crawling all over his feet and one time a pink pig walked into his quarters dressed like a four-star general.'

'Just because he hadn't slept?'

Her father curled his tongue around his front teeth and nodded. 'Apparently. You've lost a lot of sleep since we came back from holiday.'

'Yes, that's true.'

'I think that may be all that's wrong with you.'

She found it difficult to believe him, but she felt relief wash over her all the same. 'You *really* think so?'

'I really think so. I think if maybe we got you a prescription for sleeping pills – really strong pills that would knock you out and send you so deep you wouldn't dream – then my guess is the hallucinations would stop.'

'Does Mum have to know?'

'Not unless you need somebody to make a fuss of you.'

'No, I don't. Thanks, Dad.' She hesitated. 'Dad, I don't want to go to Dr Bendix.' Dr Bendix was their local GP. He'd known her since she was a baby and still treated her as if she were only four years old.

'Then you don't have to,' he said easily. 'Tell you what – I'll set up an appointment with

Paul Redmond. You'll like him and he's ideal for this.'

'Who's Paul Redmond?'

'We went to school together,' her father said. 'He trained as a general practitioner, but then went on to do psychiatry. He can give you the knock-out pills, then if that doesn't work, he's *qualified* to tell you you've gone loony-tunes.' He stood up. 'Come on, let's put the kettle on – your mother will be home in a minute and I want us to be talking about *The Archers* when she does.'

Janie took a cab from school next day with the tenner her father slipped her over breakfast and gave the address he wrote down on the card. Twenty minutes later she found Dr Redmond's name-plate outside a sedate Georgian building in a better quarter of town. She climbed the steps, pushed open the front door and found herself walking on dove-grey carpet. A chic receptionist smiled at her professionally from behind a desk of tubular steel and glass and suddenly Janie felt very young and ill at ease in her school uniform.

She felt even more ill at ease as she climbed the carpeted stairs to Dr Redmond's consulting room. ('First floor, second door,' the receptionist had said, still smiling.) But when she knocked and went in, a lot of things changed.

Dr Redmond was a teddy bear of a man who looked a few years too young to have been at school with her father. He was wearing a tweed sports jacket that made him look more like an academic than a doctor.

'Hello,' she said uncertainly, 'I'm Jane Hyde.'

'Paul Redmond.' They shook hands. His hand reminded her of Alan's hand in her hallucination. It swallowed hers.

She looked around the consulting room. It was lined with psychiatric text-books and there was an antique globe in one corner. His desk looked antique too, although it was hard to tell under the clutter of files and papers. To her amusement, she noticed *The Hitchhiker's Guide to the Galaxy* poking out from under one pile. His pictures were a surprise. They all seemed to be cartoon prints and there was one definite original, a Scarfe caricature of Redmond himself. She continued to look round.

'What are you looking for?'

'Your psychiatrist's couch,' Janie said.

'Do you want to lie on a couch?' Redmond asked. 'I can have one sent up.' He grinned, suggesting the couch wasn't the only thing to be sent up.

Janie grinned back. 'It's all right – a chair will do.'

When she sat down he walked round the desk and took a seat beside her. 'Flick tells me you're in a bit of trouble.'

She frowned at him. 'Flick?'

'Sorry – John. Your father. We used to call him Flick at school. Nightmares, stress, that sort of thing? He gave me a very brief rundown when he called last night.'

Flick? Her father was called *Flick* at school? Aloud, she said, 'Not just nightmares. Did he tell you the rest?'

Dr Redmond shook his head. 'Actually it doesn't matter what he told me. I need to hear the story from you so there's no distortion. Want to tell me?'

Janie told him. He was just as good a listener as Toby (she noticed he had several of the same mannerisms) and kept absolutely quiet until she'd finished. Then he said, 'Would you mind if I asked you a few questions?'

'Not at all.'

They turned out to be more than a few. By the time he'd finished, he'd taken a full medical history, persuaded her to talk about her parents, her friends, her sex life (*what* sex life, Janie had asked him), her school, her teachers, her toilet habits, her diet, her PMT and even, amazingly, her religion.

'So you're not a Catholic?' he asked when she'd replied to that one.

She shook her head.

'Ever been to Mass?'

'Not that I remember,' Janie said. She grinned. 'Outside of my hallucinations.' She could talk about her experiences quite openly now – he had that sort of effect on her.

Dr Redmond took notes, grunted encouragingly from time to time, but made no comment at all. Janie watched him carefully as he closed his notebook, hoping to get a hint of what he thought. When she didn't, she asked him outright.

He chewed his lower lip thoughtfully for a moment before answering. 'I'm not absolutely sure, but I think your father is probably right. You're bound to look at this whole thing in terms of your symptoms, but I need to take a broader perspective.'

'What's that mean?' Janie asked.

'Well, to you, this whole thing started on the last day of your holiday when you visited Maris Caulfield and then had the first nightmare in the car on the way home—'

'I saw the ghost before that,' Janie put in.

'The ghost isn't important. Your boyfriend's right – it's the nightmares that are troubling you. And now these waking dreams, of course.'

'That's what you think they are? Waking dreams?'

'Oh, certainly,' Dr Redmond said, as if it was the most obvious thing in the world. 'This sort of thing is far more common than people realise. Virtually everybody has an hallucination or two in their lifetime, but most of us don't notice.'

'Don't *notice*?' Janie echoed, astounded.

'You only notice hallucinations if they're odd – like yours. If you're walking through the woods, you could hallucinate a hundred trees and never notice. Why would you? People can hallucinate an ashtray on the table or a passing motor car and never know it wasn't actually there. It's only when they start to see little green men that they pay attention.'

'You mean, it's not a sign of mental illness?'

'It certainly is *sometimes*. But not all the time, not even most of the time. I'd never diagnose a patient on the basis of hallucination alone. I'd have to look for other signs. In your case they're not there, but you are under stress.'

'Stress?' Janie said flatly.

'That's what I meant about putting it into context. You told me you were tired before your holiday. Now you're back at school, you're heading into your exams in the next eight weeks. You've got a nice boy, but you worry about losing him – all girls do when they find a decent young man, but that doesn't make it any less of a strain. Then you've got the usual teenage hormone imbalances. It all adds up. I think Maris Caulfield became a focus for your stress, but I don't think it was the cause of it.'

'So what do I do?' Janie asked.

Dr Redmond stood up. 'I'm going to put you on a course of sleeping tablets, exactly as your father suggested. They're rather old-fashioned tablets, I'm afraid. They contain something called phenobarbitone. This used to be prescribed a lot for sleep disorders until they discovered it suppressed the dream function. You slept, but you didn't dream, which is generally speaking not a good idea. Except in your case it's exactly what you need for a while. It'll be a short course – not more than a week – and I want you to come back to see me when it's finished. OK?'

'OK,' Janie agreed.

As she was leaving his consulting room with the prescription for the tablets in her blazer pocket, a thought occurred to her and she turned. 'Dr Redmond, this experience of mine in the house at Maris Caulfield . . .?'

'Yes?'

'I was just wondering – do you *believe* in ghosts?'

He answered without a moment's hesitation. 'I do actually.' He grinned. 'Try not to spread it around.'

NINE

At 10.58 that evening, Janie swallowed two tiny white pills. By 11.15, she was in a place of velvet darkness far beyond the reach of any hunchback.

She felt woozy when she awoke the next morning, but the joy of sleeping without the nightmare quickly swept away the cobwebs. She took the day cautiously, alert for the possibility of another hallucination, but none came. That night she took two more pills and sank straight back into the velvet darkness.

She felt so much better on the Friday that she went to a movie with Toby and so much better after *that* she agreed to a disco on Saturday night, even though she was backed up with homework. She was so exhausted after the dance she forgot to take her pills, but the hunchback never appeared. That left her feeling high enough to say yes when Toby suggested a walk in the park on Sunday. The day was overcast with only thin sunshine, but she held his hand as they walked and felt, for the first time in weeks, that life was really, deeply *good*.

They were sitting on a bench throwing crisps

to the ducks when she decided to tell him about the hallucinations.

'Dr Redmond calls them "waking dreams",' she remarked thoughtfully as she finished. She gave a mischievous smile. 'Brought on by the stress of having a boyfriend like you.'

To her surprise, Toby said seriously, 'I'm not sure he's right.'

'Hey, come on, fella – I was only joking.'

Toby gave her a startled look, then giggled. 'I don't mean about *me*. If you think this is stress, wait till I really get going.' He leaned across and kissed her on the cheek. 'No, I meant about the waking dreams. I'm not so sure he's right about them.'

Suddenly wary, Janie said, 'You think they really were hallucinations? I mean, serious stuff like give her an injection and pass the straight-jacket, Dr Freud?'

But Toby was shaking his head. 'No, I don't mean that at all. I don't know *what* they were, but don't you think the *content* was a bit odd?'

'Content?' Janie echoed, frowning.

'The way it was so like what happened at Maris Caulfield.'

Still frowning, Janie asked, 'When I saw the ghost, you mean?'

'No, I don't mean Maris Caulfield *now*. I mean back *then*. Don't tell me you hadn't *noticed*?'

She hadn't and she still wasn't sure what he was talking about. 'You'd better spell this out. I think the pills must have rotted my brain.'

'Well, these waking dreams or whatever they are. You're not yourself in them – you're somebody else. Older. Married to this big joker, Alan. Keeping chickens somewhere in the country. Don't you think that's like Maris?'

Bewildered, Janie said, 'It's not even slightly like Maris.'

'Not Maris *now*,' Toby said again. 'Maris as it was in the fourteenth century. The village was smaller then. You lived on the outskirts – maybe even in that house you saw. It's part of the village now, but back then it would have been a little farm outside. Did the two houses look anything the same?'

'The one I saw? Look the same as the one I lived in when I had the hallucinations?' She shook her head, not in denial but frustration. 'I never saw the house I lived in when I had the hallucinations. I was in the yard or walking down the lane or across the fields or in the church, but I never actually saw the house.'

'What about the church?' Toby asked. 'Was it the same?'

'No,' Janie said, 'but then it wouldn't be. The Maris church they have today was only built about seventeen hundred.'

'Look,' said Toby, 'from what you tell me, every time you have one of these . . . what do you want me to call them: waking dreams? hallucinations?'

'Call them anything you like.'

57

'Visions,' said Toby tactfully. 'Every time you have one of these visions, you're a married woman living somewhere a lot different to where you live now.'

'That's for sure!'

'But in the last one you were talking about, there was plague in London. That has to be the fourteenth century.'

'No it doesn't,' Jane said suddenly. A fragment of a history lesson had returned to her. 'There was an outbreak of the Black Death in England in the seventeenth century. It hit London too. It was the Great Fire that stopped it then, in sixteen sixty-six.'

'All right,' Toby agreed placatingly. 'It was either the seventeenth or the fourteenth century. But didn't you say that in your last vision this guy Barnabas Whatsit—'

'Saul,' Janie murmured. 'Barnabas Saul.'

'Barnabas Saul was sick. His wife said she couldn't get him out of bed.'

'But it wasn't the Black Death,' Jane said.

'How do you know?'

She blinked. 'Well, I . . . well . . . Actually, I don't, but his wife didn't say anything about the plague. She just said he had a headache or something.'

'Barnabas Saul was the village tailor, wasn't he?' Toby asked.

'That's right.'

'Didn't you tell me it was the tailor who brought the plague to Maris Caulfield?'

Janie stared at him. 'You're right. He bought a

bolt of cloth from London and it had plague fleas in it.' A strange little shiver crawled along the base of her spine.

'There's something else,' Toby said. 'Didn't you say the priest was called Father Maris?'

'Yes, I did.'

'Maris Caulfield was called after a Father Maris who died in the plague in the fourteenth century. The original name was just Caulfield – Field of the Caul, which is a thing babies sometimes get born with over their face. They added Father Maris's name in fourteen-something because they reckoned he was a bit of a saint.'

Janie stared at him, stunned. 'How do you know?'

'I looked it up,' Toby said. 'After you told me about seeing the ghost, I looked up Maris Caulfield in the Shell Guide and then got a local history out of the library. I was sort of interested to see if there was any mention of a haunted house or something like that.'

'Wow!' Janie breathed. She couldn't think of anything else to say, although there were a lot of things she wanted to say. Like: *What does it mean?* Toby seemed to be telling her she'd been hallucinating something that really happened, more than six hundred years ago.

'You know Dr Redmond asked if you were a Catholic?' Toby said. 'I was sort of wondering about that myself . . .'

'You *know* I'm not a Catholic,' Janie said, staring at him. 'Dad's brother is a rector in the Church of England – you've *met* him!'

'No, I wasn't wondering if you were a Catholic,' Toby said. 'I was wondering how you knew so much about a fourteenth-century Mass. I expect Dr Redmond was wondering that too. You described it perfectly.'

TEN

Janie had almost managed to forget the conversation with Toby by the time she made her second visit to Dr Redmond. The sleeping pills had worked a treat. No hunchback – no dreams of any sort that she could remember – and best of all, no *waking* dreams, hallucinations, visions or whatever you wanted to call them. None at all. The worst had happened was her head was a little woolly in the mornings, but even that usually cleared up in an hour or two.

Dr Redmond was sitting on the edge of his desk reading something as she came in. He glanced up over the top of his glasses and said at once, 'You look better.'

'I feel better,' Janie told him.

'Finished your pills?'

'Sort of.' She fished the bottle out of her pocket and shook it. Something rattled lightly in the bottom. 'I forgot to take them one night, so I've two left over.'

'What was the effect of missing the dose?'

'Nothing.' Janie grinned triumphantly. 'Not that I could see anyway. I just went to sleep as usual and didn't dream.'

'Good!' said Dr Redmond. He sounded genuinely pleased.

Janie looked at him. 'What happens now?' She'd gone home from school and changed before coming for this appointment and felt a thousand per cent more self-confident out of uniform. Dr Redmond, she noticed, still favoured the academic look, although it was a different sports jacket.

'What happens now is we talk.' He waved her into a chair and sat down himself. 'Let me just make sure I've got it right. The pills worked?'

'Yes.'

'No nightmares?'

'No.'

'No waking dreams – hallucinations?'

'None.'

'But you did feel a bit listless and woozy much of the time – probably still do?'

'That's right,' Janie said. 'How did you know?'

'Common side-effect of the pills, I'm afraid,' Redmond told her. He reached into the pocket of his jacket, but brought his hand out empty. 'I wish I hadn't given up smoking,' he said. 'I miss my pipe.'

Janie grinned at him. 'Am I cured, Dr Redmond?'

'Do you know,' said Redmond, 'I think you might be.' He scratched his neck. 'We'll know for sure in a day or two. I want you to stop the pills now – throw away the two you've left. You can't stay on them for ever, but I think a week—'

'Six days,' Janie put in.

'Even six days,' said Dr Redmond, smiling, 'should be enough to break the stress pattern.' He placed his hands on his knees. 'Well, I could keep you here for another hour rattling on about your symptoms – or lack of them now, apparently – but the fact is you'll still have the drug in your system for the next forty-eight hours so you won't dream tonight or tomorrow night whatever we do.'

'What happens after tomorrow night?' Janie asked.

'Hopefully nothing. Your normal dream pattern should re-establish itself, but you shouldn't have any more nightmares. Without the nightmares it's my belief you couldn't hallucinate if you tried.'

'So the dreams and the hallucinations were tied together?' Janie asked.

Dr Redmond shook his head. 'Not directly. The nightmares wrecked your rest. The hallucinations were tied to lack of sleep. It was a sort of domino effect. Stress triggered the nightmares, the nightmares triggered lack of sleep, lack of sleep triggered the hallucinations. Now we've broken the pattern, you should have no more trouble. Especially if you try not to overdo things, which I know is very difficult at your age.' He stood up and offered his hand. 'Tell your dad it doesn't have to be an emergency before he phones me. We might arrange a poker game sometime – he usually loses.'

'I'll tell him,' Janie promised. 'Thank you, Dr Redmond.'

She closed the door and started down the stairs to reception. On the third step everything went dark.

'No!' she screamed. 'Sweet Jesus, no!'

Alan's lips were blue. A black tongue poked between them. He was shivering and sweating by turns, mumbling like a madman then shrieking in agony as another muscle spasm racked his body. He had torn his clothes so she could see the angry swellings at his armpits and his groin. They were already as large as apples and seemed to be growing larger by the minute. The skin on one of them, stretched to breaking point, had cracked minutely and an ooze of greenish-yellow pus was dribbling out.

Jayne stared down at him, scarcely able to believe her eyes. He had been *well* this morning. She'd watched him walk off to the Big House, promising in his simple, childlike way to be no more than two hours; and that because he knew she needed him about the farm. She'd not seen him return, which was no odds since she'd been busy. But then she'd happened to come into the house – and it *was* the same house, a strange part of her whispered mysteriously – and found him lying there just like the tailor.

Except Bess Saul, the tailor's wife, had come home from Mass to find Barnabas dying nigh on two weeks ago and died herself soon after. But there had been no more cases of the Blue Sickness since – none. Even Squire Burston said that God had stayed his hand and spared their village. All knew this pestilence spread like fire in the hay.

Whole towns were infected in the space of days. That none had died or even coughed since Bess Saul was a sign for sure. Barnabas and Bess had been secret sinners, so God had sought them out. But God was merciful as well as strict and the good folk of Caul Field had been spared.

Except He hadn't spared her Alan, who never did harm to nobody and was too simple to have sinned! Jayne reached out to touch his forehead and found it burning like brimstone. The movement called him from whatever hell he was lying in and his eyes turned towards her. They were glazed and filled with pain and confusion so that she doubted he knew her. But he whispered through his swollen tongue, 'Water . . .'

'Aye, Alan,' Jayne said, 'I'll fetch you water. Don't you worry none, my love, because you be going to get better.'

But when she brought the bucket from the well, he was gone, his eyes still open, rolled upwards, with a trickle of black blood at one side of his mouth.

Jayne set the bucket down and knelt beside the corpse. Her hand fumbled in her apron and took out the little wooden rosary. Her fingers stroked a bead. 'Hail Mary, full of grace, blessed art thou amongst women . . .' she prayed, her voice no louder than a murmur. But while her lips formed the words Father Maris had taught her, her mind spoke with a different voice. *Why did you do it, Holy Virgin?* she asked. *Why did you let your Son take my man from me?*

And what's to become of me now? a second

voice whispered in her mind. *How shall I run the farm with no man to help and aged parents to look after? Sweet Jesus, what have I done to you that you should be so cruel?*

For some reason she noticed a flea-bite on the back of Alan's pale hand. Tears began to stream down her cheeks as she prayed.

'Are you all right?'

Janie opened her eyes and looked up into the shocked, concerned face of Dr Redmond's receptionist. 'I've just watched my husband die.'

'Please don't try to move,' the receptionist said. 'I've called the doctor.'

'What happened?' Janie murmured. A part of her was still long ago and far away. Faintly, she heard hurrying footsteps on carpet.

'Apparently you fell down the stairs,' said Dr Redmond's reassuring voice. His face swam into view. 'Priscilla's quite right – you mustn't move for a moment.'

'He was fine this morning,' Janie said dreamily. 'I didn't know anyone could get so ill so quickly.'

'She's not making much sense,' the receptionist whispered to the doctor. 'There may be a concussion.'

'Can you straighten that leg?' Dr Redmond asked. Janie straightened it at once and made to sit up. 'No, don't try—' said Dr Redmond urgently. 'Oh well, you've done it now. Any agonising pains when you moved? Any broken ends of bones grating? Any signs of cracked ribs? What do they always ask in the movies – can you still feel your feet?'

Despite herself, Janie smiled a little. 'No, none of that. Except for the feet. I can still feel them.'

'Well,' said Dr Redmond in mock relief, 'at least your back's not broken.' He held up his hand. 'How many fingers?'

'Pardon?' Janie asked, confused.

'Do you have double vision?'

'No.'

'Any blurring?'

'No.'

'Any head pain?'

'No.'

'Do you remember hitting your head as you were falling down?'

'I don't remember falling down,' said Janie. 'Can I get up now?'

'I suppose you'd better,' Dr Redmond sighed. 'You're a very bad advert lying in a heap at the bottom of my stairs.' He became serious at once as she started to get up. 'Careful now!'

Janie stood up. She felt as if her shoulders had been bruised and there was pain in her neck and both knees, but mostly she was just feeling embarrassed. 'I'm fine,' she said.

'Perhaps you are,' Dr Redmond said, 'but I think you'd better come back up a moment, don't you?' He helped her up the stairs and into his consulting room, where he fussed her into the chair she'd left only minutes before. 'Did you trip?' he asked.

Janie shook her head.

'I was afraid of that,' Redmond said. 'Tell me the worst – another hallucination?'

'I'm afraid so.'

Dr Redmond rubbed his chin thoughtfully. 'So it wasn't stress.' He looked at her soberly. 'Well, young lady, it seems as if there's something we've been missing. How do you fancy another little holiday?'

Janie stared at him suspiciously. Some basic instinct told her she wasn't going to like what he was about to suggest. Underneath his light-hearted bedside manner, it was obvious he'd grown worried.

'I've a small private clinic – quite near Maris Caulfield, funnily enough – which I think we should take you into for a day or two, run a few tests, make sure you get enough rest, perhaps try some drug therapy that's not suitable for out-patients. What do you think?'

She thought she should take her leave of him right there and then, run not walk down those stairs and across the dove-grey carpet to the front door. But she only said, 'What about school?'

'We'll have to organise a little time off school,' he said. 'We'll also have to talk with your parents, of course. Can't do anything without their permission.'

'Suppose I say no?' Janie asked.

'Then we'll have to try another approach.'

'What other approach?'

Dr Redmond shifted uneasily. 'Honest answer? I don't know. I'd be far happier if I had you under proper observation for a while. You'd still be my patient – I'm at the clinic three mornings a week – and for the day-to-day routine you'd be under my colleague Dr Walker. You'll like her – she's a fine lady and knows her stuff.'

Janie said, 'Dr Redmond, this is some sort of mental hospital, isn't it?'

Redmond looked at her soberly. 'It's a psychiatric clinic, yes.'

Suddenly Janie felt very much afraid.

ELEVEN

It wasn't so bad. In fact, it wasn't bad at all. Janie's father drove her to Woodbridge Clinic (looking worried sick, but fighting hard to hide it) at ten o'clock next morning. Her mother had volunteered to come too, but they'd ganged up to dissuade her. Janie felt relieved. She was having enough problems being committed to a funny farm without her mother fussing.

Except she wasn't committed – she was going voluntarily. And it certainly didn't look like a funny farm.

The clinic was a series of single storey red-brick buildings set well back off the road and screened by mature trees. There was no high wall. *And no machine-gun posts!* Janie told herself angrily. What did she expect? Some sort of grim Victorian workhouse with a wall and guards on the gates? If this was to work, she was going to have to get real.

All the same, she scanned the grounds for signs of her fellow patients as her father braked the Volvo and drew up at a door marked *Reception*. She knew they had to look as normal as she did, but she still couldn't shake the feeling they'd look odd: she imagined drooling lips and beetling eyebrows and wide, staring eyes. There were people about all right – it was a sunny morning, warm and getting hot – but they all looked normal.

'Do you want to stay in the car a minute?' her father said. 'I'll slip in and find out where you're supposed to go.'

'OK,' Janie said. She sat in the car and stared around her, still trying to fight back the nervousness. A tall man in a white coat came out as her father was going in and held the door for him politely. A group of three women walked past in animated conversation. A teenager in sneakers and jeans, no older than herself, ran across the grass and disappeared into one of the other buildings.

A tap at the car window made her jump sharply – she'd been looking the other way – and she swung round to find a middle-aged woman leaning down with her nose pressed almost to the glass. Janie wound the window down warily: this one definitely looked odd.

'Hi, Janie,' the woman said with a pronounced Scots acent, 'I'm Janice Walker.'

Janie looked at her blankly for a moment, then the penny dropped. 'Oh, *Dr* Walker! Oh, I'm sorry.' She quickly wound the window down the remainder of the way.

'Do you want to come in?' Dr Walker asked. 'Your dad's doing the paper work – there's a mountain of it in places like this, I'm afraid. I thought I'd get you settled and he can come and say good-bye before he goes.'

'Yes, all right,' Janie said. She climbed out of the car. 'I've got a suitcase in the boot.'

'I'll get somebody to take care of that,' Dr Walker said. 'We've any amount of big strapping lads out here.'

To Janie's relief, she had a private room. It was smaller than her room at home, but it looked comfortable enough and had a loo and shower en suite. The big strapping lad who'd materialised dropped her case, grinned broadly, then disappeared along the corridor. Dr Walker took her in a different direction for the guided tour.

It was a lot less formal than she'd imagined, not at all an institution. When they came to the kitchens, Dr Walker remarked, 'We've got set meal-times – there's a note of them in your room – but if you feel like a snack in the middle of the night, the fridge is just through there.'

The tour ended in Dr Walker's office. The furnishings were a lot more spartan than Dr Redmond's consulting room, but the chair, Janie found, was just as comfortable.

'Well now,' said Dr Walker as she sat down, 'I think we should have a wee talk while we're waiting for your father. Paul filled me in about your case and very interesting it is. Do you think it's time travel?'

Janie blinked at her. 'I'm sorry?'

'These visions of yours – do you think they're some sort of time travel?'

For a long moment Janie wondered which of them was the patient. Then light dawned. 'Oh, I see. You're trying to find the patient's rationalis- ation for her delusional structure.'

Dr Walker stared at her, then laughed. 'Dear God, but you're a smart girl! You should be a psychiatrist!' The smile faded. 'I suppose that would be worth knowing all right, but as a matter of fact, it was an honest question. There are some very peculiar aspects to your case, you know.'

Still wary, Janie asked, 'What sort of aspects?'

'Paul and I discussed this on the phone for nearly three hours last night – *three hours*! As if I hadn't anything better to do. You're not just getting hallucinations, my girl – you're getting accurate visions of the past. Did you not suspect?'

Janie looked at her for a long time. Of course she'd suspected. She suspected she'd seen a ghost. She suspected she was being haunted in her dreams. She suspected she was living another woman's life in her visions. She suspected it was all connected with her trip to Maris Caulfield. But she only said, 'My boyfriend was trying to tell me that just the other day.'

'That's Toby, is it? Well, he's another smart one,' Dr Walker said. 'As far as I can see – well, as far as Dr Redmond can see: he's the one who's been checking it all out – every time you go into one of these wee trances of yours, you seem to be visiting the fourteenth century. Somewhere around thirteen forty-eight, to be exact.'

'How do you know?' Janie asked, suddenly excited. 'The date, I mean?'

'That's the year the Black Death reached England,' Dr Walker said.

'Dr Redmond's been checking all this? I mean, the things I saw?'

'Oh aye. He had his suspicions right from the beginning.'

'He didn't tell me!' Janie said accusingly.

Dr Walker looked at her sharply. 'You have to realise Dr Redmond's first concern is your therapy – mine too, if it comes to that. The situation you're in isn't exactly normal. It was giving you a lot of grief. And to be absolutely honest, it could have killed you – you were very lucky when you tumbled down those stairs. Paul's idea was to call a halt to the symptoms, then sort out what was happening later. Lot to be said for it.'

'I suppose so,' Janie agreed. 'But if—'

'Oh aye – if you're getting accurate visions of the past, it's a different sort of case to the man who sees pink elephants or wee green Martians. I'd agree with that all right.' She leaned forward. 'All right, Janie, cards on the table. Paul's been digging into every history book he could find. I don't know about your nightmares, but when you space out during the day, it's as if you're living another life back in thirteen forty-eight, probably as your namesake Jayne Hyde.'

'And everything I've seen is *true*?' Even though she'd suspected it, it still seemed unbelievable.

'I don't know about everything,' Dr Walker said. 'But a lot of it is. Dr Redmond and I agreed it would be best to tell you before starting your treatment here.'

Janie was still trying to adjust. 'Yes. Yes, thank you.' She shook her head. 'I didn't think you people believed in this sort of thing.'

'By *you people* I suppose you mean psychiatrists?' Dr Walker scratched her chin. 'As a breed we're far less narrow-minded than people credit. You have to be in this profession. You keep coming up against the weirdest things when you investigate the human mind. Nine shrinks out of ten accept telepathy as a matter of course. Dr Redmond believes in ghosts – did you know that? Even Freud at the end of his life said if he had it all to do again, he'd go into psychical research. Visions of the past aren't so rare and they're not necessarily all that weird.'

'They aren't?'

'Let's look at the simple possibilities first. You visit Maris Caulfield and find a house where one of the names on the plaque is close to your own – actually *is* your own if you take the old spelling into account. Our own names are very important, both at a conscious and an unconscious level: they're a prime symbol of the persona. Seeing your name as a plague victim would have made a deep impression.'

Janie said, 'Yes, I think it did. It was, sort of, you know – a shock.'

'Of course it was.' Dr Walker pulled up another chair and set it facing Janie. She sat, leaning forward. 'Now suppose, just suppose, you once read a book about Maris Caulfield—'

'I didn't,' Janie said.

'—and then, over the months or years, *forgot* you'd read it.' She smiled. 'So when your psychiatrist suggested you'd read that book, you'd tell her you didn't.'

Janie smiled back. 'Point taken,' she said. 'But I *really* don't remember reading anything about Maris Caulfield.'

'Maybe not,' said Dr Walker, 'but *if* you did, your unconscious would remember, even if you've now forgotten consciously. They've done a lot of studies and while it's hard to believe, everything we've ever read, or seen, or heard – and I mean *everything* – is stored away by the unconscious. Mostly we can't get at it, but occasionally bits pop up again.'

'You're telling me I could have got details like Father Maris and the fourteenth-century Mass and the way Jayne Hyde lived out of a book?'

'I'm telling you the unconscious mind is extraordinarily creative. If it wanted to weave a vision for you, it's quite capable of taking information from books or articles you've read and forgotten. Even old movies, television programmes – all grist to the mill.'

'So you think that's what's been happening to me?' Janie asked.

'Did I say that?' asked Dr Walker severely. 'I just said that was the simplest explanation. It's not necessarily the only explanation. Or even the true explanation. But that's what we're here to find out.'

'Look, let me get this straight—' Janie began.

But Dr Walker was rising to her feet. 'Ah, here's your dad to say his good-byes.' She walked to greet him at the door. 'Now, don't you worry about her, Mr Hyde. She's going to be absolutely fine and you can visit her just as often as you want.'

Which sounded fine, except it also sounded as if she was going to be staying at Woodbridge Clinic for quite some time.

TWELVE

The routine turned out to be OK, even restful.
Breakfast was served between 8 and 9.30, later
than she was used to getting up to go to school.
Mornings were therapy, which in Janie's case
meant talking to Dr Walker. Afternoons were
OT – Occupational Therapy – which was
Optional Therapy in Janie's case, but kind of fun
when she got bored enough to try it. Evenings
were free and the clinic had no less than seven
rooms with television sets. It even, she discovered
on her second day, had a coffee bar. Best of all,
her fellow patients weren't odd, although most
of them were withdrawn and a few were quite
depressed.

Janie expected she would be put back on the
sleeping pills, but she wasn't.

'I think the time's come to study your process,
not interfere with it,' Dr Walker said. 'Dr Redmond's idea was reasonable enough – what I'd
have done myself – but it didn't work. Now it's
important we know what we're dealing with. So
no drugs. Is that OK with you?'

Janie nodded. 'Does this mean the nightmares
will come back?'

'In all honesty I have to tell you they probably will,' Dr Walker said. 'Can you bear it?'

As it turned out she didn't have to, at least for a while. Thursday night and Friday night were both dream-free and she had no hallucinations during the day. What she did have was visits. Her father came on Thursday afternoon, bringing flowers, which was nice. Both parents turned up on Friday afternoon, bringing chocolate, which was even nicer. Her mother was so laid back Janie suspected she must be on tranquillizers, and felt a pang of guilt. It had to be difficult getting used to your daughter having mental problems.

On Friday evening, after supper, Toby came to visit. He was carrying a brown paper bag and seemed ill at ease. She noticed with amusement he was trying to avoid looking at the other patients. But his face lit up when he spotted her.

'You look great!' he said with feeling after the obligatory kiss. 'I thought they'd have doped you to the eyebrows.'

'No dope,' Janie told him. 'I'm *under observation*. They're trying to find out what's wrong with me before they'll give me so much as an aspirin. What's in the bag?'

Toby looked startled, then handed it across. 'Oh, this is for you.'

She thought it might be grapes, but when she looked inside she found it was a hamburger in a bun. She started to giggle.

'I just worried in case they weren't feeding you properly,' Toby said, looking mildly hurt.

She kissed him again with a lot of feeling. 'They're feeding me wonderfully. Gourmet style. But thanks for the thought.' She looked around. They were in one of the television lounges, which tended to get crowded in the evening. 'Want to see my room?'

'Is that an offer?' Toby asked.

'Not exactly,' Janie said. 'It's just more private to talk.' She arched an eyebrow. 'Although I *could* do with a cuddle.'

They lay on the bed and cuddled for quite a long time, but it was obvious Toby was still feeling ill at ease. Eventually he got up and sat on one of the chairs. Janie stayed on the bed, but sat up with her feet tucked under her. 'You're worried about me, aren't you?'

'I hate to admit it,' Toby said.

'Don't hate – I think it's sweet. But I'm fine. I really am.'

'I know you are. I know *really*. It's just I get this stupid idea they're setting up to fry your brains like in *One Flew Over the Cuckoo's Nest*.'

'I know,' Janie said. 'I didn't tell anybody, but I was scared stiff coming in here. I thought I'd be surrounded by nutters eating, like, *flies*. And doctors with big hands and Viennese accents. "Holt her down, Sister, und ve will amputate ze brain." But it's not like that at all. Janice is a sweetie and—'

'Who's Janice?'

'The mad Dr Walker from Glasgow. She's looking after me here, although I'm due to see

Dr Redmond tomorrow – he's got some sort of business interest in the clinic and he works here two or three days a week. Or mornings, or afternoons or something – I'm not sure. Anyway, I'm seeing him tomorrow. The interesting thing is—'

'Can I talk to you about this business?' Toby cut in. He looked serious to the point of misery and she felt suddenly very sorry for him. But hard on the heels of that feeling came another: a tingle of fear. Was he about to tell her their relationship was over? It hadn't occurred to her before that moment, but suddenly she realised it would make sense. Who wanted a girlfriend with hallucinations, locked up – well, not exactly *locked* but who worried about details? – in a psychiatric clinic?

With her throat suddenly tight, Janie said, 'OK.'

'You remember what I was saying to you last weekend?'

With her mind still on the possibility of a break-up, Janie said, 'You said a lot to me last weekend.'

'In the park,' Toby said. 'About your . . . visions.'

She didn't like the way he hesitated before he said 'visions'. He'd been about to say 'hallucinations' and while she'd told him she didn't care what he called them on Sunday, she certainly cared what he called them now. Not trusting herself to speak, she simply nodded.

But suddenly it was all right. Toby was saying,

'You know I thought what you were seeing was connected with Maris Caulfield?'

Janie said, 'Yes.'

'Well, I wasn't sure about it then – I mean, it only seemed odd you'd managed to get so many facts rights – but I've been back to the library since, back a couple of times actually, and I had a half-day on Wednesday so I went up to Maris Caulfield—'

'You *went* to Maris Caulfield? How on earth did you get there?'

He looked at her, surprised. 'Took the train,' he said. 'What's the big deal?'

Flustered, Janie said, 'I don't know. I mean, I just didn't expect you to go there, that's all. I mean, *why*?'

'I wanted to have a look at the local records. You know, see if there was anything we should know about Jayne Hyde – I mean the old Jayne Hyde who lived in Maris Caulfield at the time of the Black Death.'

'I *know* who you mean!' Janie said. She felt a sudden welling of delight. He'd gone to Maris to try to *help* her!

'Anyway, I got to talking to the rector. Nice old character called Canon Beattie. He's very much the local historian and Maris being a plague village he's made a sort of speciality of the time of the Black Death. Once he started, I couldn't shut him up. He told me the whole story of how the plague reached the village and who got sick and when and how long they lasted before they died. Everything. When it comes to detail, the man is absolutely amazing. Anyway, the point is, you haven't just been getting a few things right in your visions, you've been getting *everything* right. Every last thing.'

'Toby—'

'For example,' Toby said, his excitement increasing, 'you said you were married to this man Alan. Well, you could have got that off the plaque. But you said he was a bit of a simpleton and Canon Beattie mentioned the same thing. Apparently there'd been some trouble at his birth which left him a bit, you know . . .' Toby got up, sat on the edge of the bed and took her hand. 'Absolutely everything you said about the people and the place was accurate. Alan, your husband, was the third person in the village to die of the plague after the tailor and his wife.'

'I know,' Janie said.

He blinked. 'You do?'

'I saw him die in the vision that made me fall down the stairs.'

'That proves it, then!' Toby exclaimed.

'Proves what?'

'You're not going batty!'

Despite herself, Janie grinned. 'Did you think I was?'

'No, of course not, but you know what I mean. Listen, I think I know what's going on.'

Janie sighed theatrically. 'I'm glad somebody does.'

'No, this is important,' Toby told her earnestly. 'If we know what's going on, we can do something about it. If we don't, they're going to keep you here for ever and try every type of treatment and it won't make any difference.'

That made sense. Janie said quietly, 'What's going on, Toby?'

And Toby said, 'I think you're being haunted.'

THIRTEEN

When Janie reported to Dr Walker's office next morning, she found Dr Redmond already there. He seemed genuinely pleased to see her and shook her hand warmly. To her surprise, he was wearing a sober grey suit. 'You look well,' she ventured.

He smiled broadly. 'They won't let me into this place unless I dress respectably.'

Behind them, Dr Walker bustled in. 'Ah, you're here, Paul. Good morning. Good morning, Janie. Sorry I'm a wee bit late – Emily Collis collared me.' She threw her eyes to heaven, indicating that to be collared by Emily Collis was a fate worse than death.

'Well, now,' said Dr Walker, 'have you been filling Paul in on progress?'

Janie frowned. 'I didn't know there was any.'

Both doctors burst into spontaneous laughter. 'Well,' said Dr Redmond, 'that's put you in your place, Janice.'

'I'm sorry,' Janie said at once. 'I didn't mean it like—' She shook her head.

'Of course you didn't, Janie!' Dr Walker said, still grinning. 'Don't tease the girl, Paul – she's got enough to cope with at the moment.'

'First things first,' said Dr Redmond. 'Is the food even half decent?'

'It's very good,' Janie told him.

'Never mind the bedside manner,' Dr Walker said, her accent more acute than ever. 'This wee girl has had no nightmares since she came here, no hallucinations since she came here.' She looked at Dr Redmond underneath her eye-brows. 'And no drugs of any sort since she came here.'

'What has she had?' asked Dr Redmond.

'Two hours psychotherapy each morning for the past two days.'

There was some sort of hidden agenda between these two, Janie thought. Maybe it was a difference of opinion on her treatment. She was interested in Dr Walker's comment about psychotherapy. She'd reported to Dr Walker's office for the past two mornings and chatted about her health and her family and her school and her life in a very relaxed manner. But though the sessions were officially called therapy, she really hadn't thought of them as *psycho* therapy.

'Mmm,' said Dr Redmond thoughtfully. He turned to Janie.

'God's curse upon FitzGerald,' her father muttered, softly spoken for once. But others heard and took it up. It was Sheriff FitzGerald who posted men upon the roads and ordered any from Caul Field to be driven back by pike and sword. Had it not been for him they could have fled this accursed place as soon as Bess Saul found her husband Barnabas a-dying. For two weeks after there had been not a hint of sickness – two weeks when all could have fled the plague. Too late now, thanks to FitzGerald and his sour-faced men.

As the muttering became a growl, Father Maris spoke up. 'The Sheriff will answer to God on the Day of Judgement, Rob Willis. We needs look to our own sins.'

Our own sins, Jayne echoed in her head. *And what sins did my man commit?* Alan was dead ten days now and there was not a one in Caul Field thought on him save her. The fear was too great and there was scarce a family left did not have a cousin or uncle dead of the plague, if it was not a brother dead or a wife dead or a husband dead like her own. And still FitzGerald would not give leave for the healthy to leave the village. Her father was right, whatever the priest said. God's curse upon the man!

She looked over at Joss Higgs, wringing his hands beside the grave. His wife Mary, a cheerful soul, was beneath the ground. *What sins did Mary commit? Did she blaspheme, she who could never find an ill word even for a beggar?* Mary had died hard, her lips blue, black blotches on her skin, the swellings in her armpits and her groin like bunches of angry plums. She had died screaming, her empty eyes on Hell, not knowing Joss or their son Samuel, or their daughter who was called Mary too. *What sins did that good woman commit that she deserved so dread a punishment?*

It seemed that half the village was gathered in

the churchyard to bury Mary Higgs and pray with her husband and her children. But there were notable gaps in the crowd. Tom Cartwright was there without his Jennet. Hal Dale was absent as was his eldest boy Tom. Peter Wake was missing. So was Betsy Coke. Except they weren't missing. They were all with Mary Higgs, deep underground. They were all blue from the plague and swollen from the plague and dead from the plague, along with scores more like them. *What sins did they commit, these decent folk of Caul Field?*

Sickened by the thought, Jayne started to move away. How long would it be before she joined Alan? How long would it be for her father and her mother? How long would it be for any of them?

Father Maris recommended prayer, but Jayne was no longer as sure of God's sweet mercy as she once had been. Prayer hadn't helped Jennet Cartwright who was on her knees continuously since the disease took her uncle and who fell from her knees in a fever when the plague took her. Prayer hadn't helped Joseph Mason, who was taken on his way to church. Aye, and prayer hadn't helped Squire Burston, for all his money and the Masses that he paid for. They were all dead now, every one, bloated, swollen, pus-filled corpses laid like Mary Higgs beneath the ground.

'They say it might be witchcraft,' whispered young Luke Fisher the blacksmith's son. He had been watching the burial with strangely placid eyes.

'Oh aye,' said Jayne shortly, her expression sour. She feared the malice of witches as much as the next woman, but this was no souring of the milk or a failing of the crop. This was pestilence, no softer word for it, and pestilence was God's work, pure and simple.

The thought struck her that the churchyard was near full, not of the living, but of the dead. The pestilence had claimed so many these past ten days, there would soon be no place to bury them. Jayne shuddered. Whatever you thought about God's mercy, all knew you must be laid to rest in hallowed ground else you lost all chance of Heaven.

She moved away a little further. Despite her doubts, there was comfort in the graveyard, comfort in the shadow of the church, but against that had to be weighed the misery on the faces of her friends, the creeping terror, the darting glances as each wondered who would be the next to go.

By the graveside, Father Maris stopped his Latin muttering.

If she went now, she could start dinner early. All needed to eat hearty at a time like this, however they felt, in order to keep up their strength. Especially ageing parents. And God knew there was no shortage of food, more now than she ever remembered. For while Sheriff FitzGerald let none out of Caul Field, he caused provisions to be placed on the road into the village. Armed men set down the sacks and the barrels, then retreated back with watchful eyes.

The villagers came out and carried them in. Every second day there was something. And the Sheriff was generous in his quantities, perhaps more generous than he knew, for now there were fewer and fewer mouths to feed. Those who remained ate well, if they had the appetite.

'I don't believe on it myself,' Luke Fisher said, still prattling about witchcraft. He wanted to talk, on account of his loneliness. His mother had died giving him life and he had been raised by his father. But his father, big strapping man, strongest in the village, was the next to die after her Alan. She'd seen the corpse and wondered at how shrunken he looked. Now young Luke fended for himself.

'Come eat with us after,' Jayne said on a sudden impulse. 'There be plenty.'

'Thankee, Ma'am,' Luke said promptly. 'You be a kindly woman.' He smiled (the first smile she'd seen in the village for over a week) and looked then the image of his father. 'I'll come when I be finished my business, if that be to your liking.'

Jayne nodded. Everyone in the village knew his 'business'. He was sweet on a girl named Martha Hepwhite from Troob. Since Fitz-Gerald's men wouldn't let her past, the girl climbed the ridge of an evening and Luke stared moony up at her like a lovesick cow. 'You come when you please.'

But he was no longer listening. 'What's the matter with the priest?'

Jayne looked. Father Maris had his head in his

hands and was bent over as if in pain. There was a stir of excited conversation round the churchyard. As she watched, the priest – *who was supposed to be a saint: what sins had he committed, God?* – tumbled forward into the open grave where the body of Mary Higgs lay.

The congregation surged forward like a living thing. Those in front stared down into the hole. A woman began keening. A man turned to one side and vomited copiously on to the ground.

'It be the sickness!' someone said. 'The Black Death has taken the priest!'

But not yet, Jayne thought. From the open grave she could hear the first ghastly, gurgling groan. Father Maris had begun the racking task of dying.

'It's taken the priest!' another whispered and another. The word spread like wildfire and with it a hideous panic. Kate Horn broke and ran, then Jake Grubb the wheelwright, then May Wills, Sam Harte, Will Brewster and Jan Miller, the baker. In seconds, the whole congregation were scattering as if the Devil himself had emerged from Hell to claim them.

In moments, only Jayne and the boy Luke were left. Even her parents had fled on their tottery feet. She stood staring across the churchyard. In the open grave, embraced by the putrid corpse of Mary Higgs, Father Maris moaned.

FOURTEEN

'Who's to hear our Confessions and take away our sins,' Jayne asked, 'now the priest's gone and FitzGerald will let no other through to replace him? Who's to say the Last Rites? Who's to bury us in hallowed ground?'

She was standing outside in the darkness, night scents all around her, asking questions of the moon. The moon was round and full and like a face; and as she watched, it became two moons, two faces. The faces were the faces of Drs Redmond and Walker, their heads together like lovers.

Dr Redmond turned to look at Dr Walker. 'Fascinating!' he murmured. 'Have you seen her do this before?'

'Didn't I tell you, she's had no symptoms since she came here.' Dr Walker's Scots voice seemed to come from a long distance. 'Besides, you're the one who's supposed to have seen it happen before.'

'I only saw her *after* it happened, at the bottom of the stairs,' Dr Redmond said. 'But that was obviously a momentary thing – nothing like this.'

'Excuse me,' Janie said angrily, 'but does the patient get a look-in here?'

They turned back towards her and Dr Redmond smiled. 'Sorry.' Both faces withdrew a little.

She was still sitting in the same chair. She hadn't moved at all so far as she could tell, except to slump sideways a little. She straightened up. 'I went off again,' she said.

'Indeed you did,' Paul Redmond said. 'One of the most interesting things I've seen in years.'

'What happened?'

Redmond turned to Walker. 'Trance? Would you say it was trance?'

'I'd certainly say it was trance,' Dr Walker told him. They both turned back to Janie.

'You talked,' said Dr Redmond. He looked pleased with the development.

'Did I?' Janie asked foolishly.

'Are you feeling all right, my dear?' Dr Walker asked.

'Never better,' Janie said, a little sourly. That was the odd thing. These visions – or call them hallucinations and face up to the reality – never left her feeling ill, or dizzy, disorientated or even mildly spacy. Except for the one time when she'd fallen down the stairs, she had no ill effects whatsoever. It was as if a switch flicked in her head and she was somewhere else. Some*when* else, to be strictly accurate. Then, a little later, the switch flicked again and she was back.

One thing she'd noticed though. Her stays in the other place were getting longer.

'How long was I out?' she asked.

Dr Redmond glanced at his watch. His eyebrows lifted. 'Good Lord, it was more than twenty minutes! Didn't seem like it.'

It seemed longer to Janie. To her it had felt like most of a day. But she only said, 'What's happening to me? Do you know yet?'

Dr Walker shook her head. 'Not exactly. But you'll be relieved to hear one thing – we can rule out hallucination. You weren't seeing little green men who weren't there. You were in a trance. That's a different thing altogether.' She walked to her desk, pushed a button on the intercom and said into a sudden crackle of static, 'Could you bring us up three cups of coffee and make them really strong – we need the caffeine.'

'Is it?' Janie asked. She caught Dr Walker's blank expression and added, 'A different thing altogether?'

'Oh yes,' Dr Redmond put in. 'An hallucination usually means a crossed wire somewhere, even when it isn't serious. Trance is a shift in consciousness. It's also part of the *normal* functioning of the human brain. You see it in every primitive culture in the world. You see it in charismatic religions. You see it at pop concerts – heavy beat, flashing lights and the kids are in another space. So your experience is normal in a sense. What fascinated me was the wealth of detail.'

'How do you know?'

'You talked – I told you.'

Janie said, 'You mean I described what was happening to me?'

'Most of it. Not all – there were times when you went completely silent: dreadfully frustrating. But you talked a great deal, described the graveyard scene and all that sort of thing. Do you remember any of it now?'

'Quite clearly,' Janie said. That was the difference between her . . . she supposed she'd have to call them *trances* now . . . between her trances and her dreams. Dreams faded. Even the nightmare of the hunchback fuzzed around the edges given time. But what she saw in her trances stayed as fresh and clear as if it were a physical memory.

'Ah, here's the coffee,' Dr Walker said. She went to the door and took a tray from somebody outside. She carried it to Janie first. 'Help yourself to milk and sugar.'

'Thanks,' said Janie gratefully. As she sipped the coffee she asked, 'Do you have any ideas yet what to do about it?'

A glance passed between them and she knew there was something they weren't telling her. Dr Redmond said carefully, 'We've had one or two ideas.'

Dr Walker said, 'We wanted to see exactly what was happening before we tried anything else. To make sure we'd be doing the right thing.'

'And do you know exactly what's happening now?' Janie pressed.

Dr Walker caught something in her tone and said, 'Not entirely.' She waited, looking at Janie.

But Janie turned to Dr Redmond. She had been wondering how to do this and now she was just going to do it anyway. 'My boyfriend thinks I'm being haunted.' Then, because she didn't want to avoid responsibility, she added, 'I think he's right.'

She wasn't quite sure what she expected. Dr Redmond had said he believed in ghosts and Dr Walker had confirmed it, although she hadn't said she believed in them herself. At the same time they were both psychiatrists. She couldn't imagine they'd simply grab the idea and run with it. And even if they did, where would they run *to*? They were psychiatrists, for heaven's sake, not Ghostbusters.

'Haunted?' echoed Dr Walker.

Janie wasn't sure she should have started this. But since she had, she'd no option but to go on. She licked her lips. 'Toby was here last night and we talked about it a lot. He's been to Maris Caulfield and talked to the rector. I know you've been reading up on the stuff I've seen, Dr Redmond, and I know you think a lot of it is accurate. But Toby thinks it's *all* accurate. Every detail.'

'Perhaps he's right,' Dr Redmond murmured.

'But he also thinks the *reason* it's so accurate is that it's not coming from me. I mean, it's not stuff I read in a book and forgot like Dr Walker thinks—'

'Only one possibility,' Dr Walker said.

'—or some sort of pyschic vision or anything like that. Toby thinks it's accurate because it's not coming from me at all. It's coming from the original Jayne Hyde. The one who lived in the fourteenth century.'

'In other words, it's coming from a ghost,' Dr Redmond said. 'I don't think that's very likely.'

Janie looked at him in surprise. 'I thought you *believed* in ghosts!'

'Yes, I do,' Redmond said. 'But I think I'd better explain what I mean by ghosts. I don't believe in spirits of the dead coming back to talk to the living – or haunt them for that matter. I don't think that's remotely possible. But at the same time, there's overwhelming evidence for ghosts. Thousands of people have seen them. Grey ladies in old castles, the thing at Hampton Court Maze. I don't believe for a moment all those people are mistaken or deluded or insane.'

'Then you *do* believe ghosts exist!'

'I just told you I did,' Dr Redmond said. 'I'm quite sure *something*'s there. What we're talking about now is exactly what that something *is*. I think it's a video recording.'

'Pardon?'

'I think,' said Dr Redmond, 'certain events, certain images can sometimes burn themselves into their surroundings. Maybe it's to do with an electrical field. Maybe it's a natural property of certain types of stone. Maybe it happens when there's a high level of emotion involved, as in a murder or a suicide. Or maybe it just gets burned in gradually, say when a monk walks the same cloisters at the same time day after day. But once it's burned in, it's ready to replay. And when it *does* replay, then you see a ghost. But it's not a spirit – it's a natural tape recording of the past.'

'Do you think that's what I've been doing?' Janie asked. 'Replaying a recording of what happened during the plague at Maris Caulfield?'

'I think you could be.'

It didn't make sense. The natural-recording theory might have explained the woman she saw in the bedroom of the house at Maris, but what about the rest? How did those visions get recorded at her school, or Dr Redmond's office, or right here in this very room?

But before she could protest, Dr Walker said, 'I'm not sure I believe in ghosts at all – not even Paul's funny tape recordings. But it does occur to me if your boyfriend's right and the spirit of the old Jayne Hyde really *is* involved, then one of the treatments we discussed might prove quite useful.' She gave Dr Redmond a meaningful glance.

'What's the treatment?' Janie asked quietly.

Dr Redmond frowned slightly. 'We were considering the use of hypnosis.'

'Providing you agree, of course,' Dr Walker put in.

'Can Toby be here when it happens?' Janie said without a moment's hesitation.

FIFTEEN

That night Janie Hyde crossed the boundary between her trance visions and her sleeping nightmare.

She went to her room at eleven, brushed her teeth, pulled on a warm nightie and climbed into bed. She lay for a moment looking at the ceiling, then reached for the bedside light. As she did so, she found herself in Caul Field.

Jayne stood outside the closed door of the bedroom listening to the sudden silence. Tears streaked the filth of her cheeks, but she felt no sorrow. She felt nothing at all. There was a physical numbness that had started in her heart and was now spreading throughout her entire body.

The silence grew.

Eventually Jayne opened the door.

Even though she knew they must be dead, even though she had seen them no more than minutes before, she was not prepared for what she saw now. The bodies of her parents were black and so bloated as to be almost unrecognisable. They lay side by side in death as they had so often in life, but the pestilence had made them strangers to each other and to her. They were like creatures from some brimstone pit, gigantic festering maggots with peeling skin and oozing sores. Their eyes were open, but they did not look at one another. Instead they were locked upwards, fastened on to Heaven as if pleading to the sweet Lord for mercy.

The numbness protected her. She walked across the room, reached down and gently closed her mother's eyes, then her father's eyes. 'Good-bye, Mother, good-bye, Father.' For some reason she found herself remembering her childhood, a particular day of autumn colours, russet and citrine, when her father, who had been so young then, ran with her across the fields. She pushed the memory away. She had work to do.

She went downstairs, through the yard and into the field where she harnessed Father Maris's donkey. With its master dead, the beast had taken to wandering wheresoever it could find grazing. She led him to the yard and yoked him to the cart. She threw in the great wooden spade, then tethered the beast and walked back into the house.

The numbness sank roots into her soul like a hard winter. She lifted her father first and was astonished at how light he had become in death. The smell of his sickness made her gag, but she controlled the reflex and half carried, half dragged him downstairs and out on to the cart. Numbly she returned for her mother. Yellow pus oozed on to her hands as she slid them beneath her mother's armpits. She closed her mind to what was happening and repeated the journey she had made with her father.

Jayne sat on the wooden seat and whipped up the donkey. The cart jerked as he plodded off.

She had scarce the need to guide him, for he walked towards the village and straight for the church. She turned him aside into the graveyard where he drew to a natural halt. Jayne climbed down from the cart.

The grave was still open. None had returned to the churchyard since the day the Lord had stricken the priest in the performance of his office. They said it was a sign, ill luck, a judgement, a warning. Perchance it was, but the churchyard remained hallowed ground, the only hallowed ground in the village.

One after the other, Jayne dragged her parents to the open grave and tipped them in. She tried not to look at the decomposing horrors of the priest and Mary Higgs already there. She said the Pater Noster, or as much of it as she could remember in her numbness, followed by three Hail Marys and a Glory Be. It was a poor service, but it was the best she could offer. She walked back to the cart, found the spade and returned painfully to fill in the grave. It was the last plot left. There was no more room for the dead in hallowed ground.

When she had finished, she walked numbly from the graveyard. Her hands were split and bleeding, but she scarcely noticed. The village streets were empty, as if everyone had already died, but she knew there were still a gross or more left, hiding in their houses from the wrath of the Lord.

What would happen now, she wondered, *now that the graveyard was full? Where would the bodies be buried for any hope of resurrection?* It was not a recent problem. Every house in Caul Field now had at least one rotting corpse. But with her parents gone, the last remaining space filled up (and that only because she had ignored the superstitions of her neighbours) it was a pressing problem. Soon she too would be taken by the fever. Soon she too would be a bloated corpse. Jayne knew it with absolute certainty. She no longer believed in the Lord's mercy. But when she was gone, who would seek out the hallowed ground to bury *her*?

She wandered aimlessly until she happened on Luke Fisher. The boy was squatted on the pavement, back against a wall, conscientiously whittling a stick. He looked up at her with large, liquid eyes. 'Good morrow, Goodwife Hyde.'

She stared at him without answering. He seemed fit and well, a broad-shouldered boy, well-muscled like his father. Why had the Lord spared him when so many were taken? Luke was not the worst of boys, but there were better than him raving in the gloom of their homes or staring with sightless eyes towards a hopeless Heaven.

'Be the roads still blocked?' she demanded peremptorily. She was still thinking of the problem of the bodies.

'Oh aye,' Luke said.

'Come with me to be certain,' Jayne commanded.

He stood up without a word and walked with

her. They passed only Arthur Harper on the streets, but his eyes were full of fever and he did not greet them.

On the road outside the village, they saw the Sheriff's men. There was a company of archers with them now. 'Go back!' called the Sergeant at Arms. 'None may leave the Caul Field. Fitz-Gerald's orders.' Without being told, the archers notched arrows to their bows.

Luke took her arm gently and led her back. As they reached the outskirts of the village she began to cry. 'Who will bury our dead?' she sobbed. She turned to grip him by the shoulders and stared into his liquid eyes. 'They confine us, they condemn us, but who will bury our dead?'

To her surprise, he answered her directly. 'Sheriff sends us a pall.' But while she heard his words, she did not understand them. Still gripping his shoulders, still staring into those brown eyes, Jayne crossed the boundary.

She was on the winding road. 'And behold a pale horse,' the familiar rasping voice whispered. Her lips moved as she chanted the words along with him: 'And his name that sat on him was Death, and Hell followed with him.'

As if the words were a conjuration, she saw the hunchback with his cart. He limped towards her, his face strangely gentle. While he was still a distance from her, he drew a handbell from beneath his tattered cloak. 'Bring out your dead!' he called and rang the bell. 'Bring out your dead!'

The hunchback approached her with his odd rolling gait. He smiled, showing long, rotted teeth like those of an ancient horse. 'I be the one to look after thee, Goodwife Hyde, and all others like thee. I be the pall FitzGerald sent.'

She did not understand, but she was no longer afraid when the creature took her hand. 'Come, Mistress,' he said, tugging gently. 'Come see what I have in my cart.'

This time she went with him, if not willingly at least with resignation. She felt tired, too tired to fight any more.

'They despise me,' the hunchback whispered. 'They fears me and some hates me.' His mouth fell open into a rot-toothed grin. 'But now they needs me, every one.'

She was not sure she understood that either, but understanding was dawning. Even through her tiredness and her numbness, she began to feel the fear.

They reached the cart.

'They're all in here, you know,' the hunchback said. 'Rich and poor, proud and humble, they all comes at the end times to my cart.'

He pulled away the sacking.

His cart was piled with corpses. They writhed and twitched and crawled and oozed. The stench of their sores rose up in a mute plea to Heaven.

Jayne stared. Her own corpse lay half-naked on the top of the pile, black and bloated like the bodies of her parents, cracked lips back in a hideous grimace of death.

Janie began to scream.

SIXTEEN

'What do you think it means?' Janie asked. It was Sunday and though she was not due a therapy session, she had requested one. She suspected she looked dreadful. She certainly felt it. Just *telling* Dr Walker her experiences of the night before had proved harrowing.

Dr Walker stared at her for a moment. 'Look, I do have one or two ideas – so does Dr Redmond – but it's a complicated business. I'm not sure I can explain it all that clearly.'

'Try,' Janie snapped. She felt frightened and the fear had shortened her patience.

If Dr Walker took offence it did not show. 'All right,' she said. She ran her tongue thoughtfully across her top lip. 'Let's review what's happened. You're on holiday with your parents, you visit Maris Caulfield, a plague village. You find a house there with your own name listed as one of the plague victims. You have an experience in the house which is similar to seeing a ghost. After that, you have a series of nightmares and trance experiences related to the plague times at Maris – since last night we know the hunchback is all part of the same pattern. Is that a fair enough summing up?'

Janie nodded. 'Yes.'

'Possibility One – and we've mentioned this to you before,' said Dr Walker. 'Seeing your name on the list of the dead was a much greater shock than you consciously realised. It was a reminder of your own mortality – of the fact that even you would die one day. This tapped into your unconscious anxieties—'

'I have unconscious anxieties?' Janie asked.

Dr Walker smiled bleakly. 'We *all* have unconscious anxieties. This tapped into them and your unconscious mind has been presenting these anxieties in dramatised form – nightmares, trance visions – ever since.'

'I didn't see my name on the list until *after* I saw the ghost,' Janie said.

'Which brings me to Possibility Two,' said Dr Walker smoothly. 'You saw the ghost – and let's not worry about whether this was a spirit of the dead or one of Paul's tape recordings or whatever: the fact is you had an experience that was perfectly real to you and consequently very shocking. Almost immediately afterwards, you saw your name on the plaque. This compounded the shock. The combination of these two traumatic experiences tapped into your unconscious anxieties—'

'So it all comes back to unconscious anxieties?' Janie said.

'I'm afraid so.'

'That wasn't so difficult,' Janie said.

'That wasn't the difficult part,' Dr Walker told her. 'The difficult part is finding out where your unconscious anxieties come from and how to deal with them.'

'Oh,' Janie said.

'It seems to me that if you want to sum up the symbolism of the nightmares and the trance visions, if you want to give it a sort of overall interpretation, that is, I'd have to say it was fear of illness, or fear of death.' Dr Walker hesitated then added, 'Or both.'

'I'm a bit young to be afraid of death, wouldn't you say?'

'It may not be your own death,' Dr Walker said. She got up and walked over to the window. Outside, a steady drizzle had driven away the usual strollers from the grounds. She turned back to Janie. 'One of the big problems of medicine – ordinary medicine, psychiatric medicine, it doesn't matter – is how much to tell the patient. Do you tell them they might have some dreadful disease and worry them sick? Or do you avoid telling them and give them no chance to help in their own cure? You see the problem?'

Janie nodded. 'Yes.' She wondered where this was leading.

'There are no guidelines from the Medical Association. There can't be, because there's no right or wrong answer. It depends on the individual case. You're young, Janie – you must have noticed you're a lot younger than most of the patients we have here. Rightly or wrongly, doctors tend to tell young people as little as possible, on the theory that they haven't the experience to handle the problems.' Dr Walker drew a long breath. 'However, you're a highly intelligent young woman and you strike me as being very mature for your age—'

'Thank you.'

'You're welcome. So I propose to be as open with you as possible. The unconscious mind isn't stupid. If it has a fear of illness, a fear of death, there's a reason.'

'What sort of reason?'

'Well,' said Dr Walker, 'that's just what I'm coming to. Sometimes when you get ill, the unconscious knows about the problem before symptoms start to show.'

'So I could be ill – physically ill – and not know it?'

'You could be,' Dr Walker said. 'Frankly, I don't think so – you look as healthy as a horse to me – but we need to check it out. I'd like you to have a full, thorough, medical examination. Dr Hilliard will carry it out: she's not just the best we have here, she's one of the best in the country. As I said, and I can't stress this strongly enough, I don't expect her to find anything. But if there's anything *to* find, she won't miss it.'

'When am I to have the examination?' Janie asked with a degree of trepidation.

Dr Walker glanced at her watch. 'You're booked to see Dr Hilliard at eleven. I'd like you to come and see me again this afternoon and we'll talk some more.'

Dr Hilliard proved to be another Scot, a tiny, matronly, grey-haired woman who was the most chillingly efficient human being Janie had ever met. She took temperature, blood pressure, listened to her heart, drew no fewer than seven blood samples (but so expertly Janie never felt a thing), organised a set of X-rays and asked endless questions, many of which dealt with family medical history.

It was lunch-time before she was finished and Janie staggered off to the dining room with the feeling of having just been fed through a mincer. At 2.30pm, she was back with Dr Walker.

'Nothing wrong, according to the preliminary report,' Dr Walker said at once.

'Preliminary?' Janie echoed with emphasis.

'We process X-rays in the clinic and three of the seven blood tests. I have the results and all these are clear. The other four blood tests go to an outside lab and we'll have the results probably on Tuesday, just possibly late tomorrow afternoon. We won't have them today, because only idiots like us work on a Sunday. But those blood tests are designed to show up conditions that are extremely rare and would almost certainly have thrown up other symptoms, so I think I can safely repeat what I said to you earlier: apart from your asthma, you're as healthy as a horse. Dr Hilliard agrees, incidentally.'

'So where does that leave us?' Janie asked.

'Well, if your unconscious isn't worried about *you*, maybe it's worried about somebody close to you.'

'You mean like Toby?'

'More likely to be one of your parents,' Dr

Walker said. 'Either of them had any serious illness lately? Either of them any problems you might worry about? Heart condition, high blood pressure, cholesterol build-up, that sort of thing?'

'Not that I know of.'

'Is there anything about them that concerns you?'

Janie thought for a moment. 'Mum's pretty stressed. She fusses a lot. But I don't think I really *worry*. I mean, I don't think she's going to keel over or anything.'

'What about the extended family? How are your grandparents?'

'Dad's mum and dad live in Miami. They're fine so far as I know: we don't see them very often. Mum's dad was killed before I was born in an accident in a machine shop. Gran's eighty-five now and everybody says she's healthier than the rest of us put together – she still goes horseback riding.'

'Doesn't seem to be that, then. Any sick friends?'

Janie shook her head. 'No.'

'You mentioned Toby . . .'

'Only because I thought you meant I might be worried about somebody like Toby. He's not sick or anything.'

Dr Walker sighed. 'All right, we've more or less eliminated those lines of inquiry. That leaves the tricky one.'

'What's the tricky one?'

'Something that happened to you in childhood.

Something that worried you so much you just wanted to forget it. And did forget it, maybe all too well.'

'Something to do with death or illness?'

Dr Walker nodded. 'Yes.'

'Well, if I wanted to forget, I wouldn't remember it now, would I? So how do we get at it?'

'Normally through a lengthy process of analysis, but you're in a bit too much immediate trouble for that. That's why Dr Redmond suggested hypnosis. Sometimes it allows us to slip past the barriers the unconscious sets up.'

Janie said seriously, 'Dr Walker, I've already agreed to hypnosis. I'd try anything. I just want to know when we can get started – today? tomorrow? The sooner the better!'

But Dr Walker was frowning. 'Well, since you're under eighteen, we need your parents' permission—'

'They'll agree,' Janie said confidently. 'I know they will.'

'Yes, they probably will, but one or both of them will have to come in and sign the papers, which will probably mean a day or two. Then it has to be a day that suits Dr Redmond – and indeed myself. Hypnosis is quite time-consuming, so we'll have to juggle other appointments. And then you want Toby present – which I think is a very good thing incidentally. It means you'll feel far more secure and relax much more easily.'

'So where does that leave us?' Janie asked anxiously.

Dr Walker shrugged. 'I'm afraid we're probably talking about next weekend – say, Saturday morning.'

Janie closed her eyes. The nightmares and the trances had become almost unendurable to her now. She wasn't sure she could hold out till Saturday.

SEVENTEEN

There were no more trances, but the nightmare came again on Sunday night, Monday night and Tuesday night. But by Tuesday night it didn't matter, because on Tuesday afternoon Dr Walker sent Janie a message that the hypnotic treatment had been arranged for the following afternoon. Her father had signed the necessary papers and returned them by courier. Dr Redmond and Dr Walker herself had reorganised their schedules. Even Toby was going to make it: Wednesday was his half-day.

Janie received the news with a flooding of relief. She was now so exhausted from lack of sleep that the world around her was turning grey and listless. She found herself dozing off over meals, while watching television, once even while *walking*. It was the weirdest sensation. One moment she was strolling through the grounds, the next she was at the tennis court. She assumed she'd dropped off and walked the rest of the way fast asleep.

On Tuesday when the nightmare came, she was almost beyond caring. She sank on to the bed and at once, it seemed, she heard the whispered words, 'And I looked, and behold a pale horse: and his name that sat on him was Death, and Hell followed with him.' Next morning when she woke, she assumed she'd had the rest of the familiar nightmare, but could remember nothing of it. Only the words remained, repeating and repeating in her head like a catchy song. They were still there when she bumped into Dr Walker.

'It sounds like a quotation,' Dr Walker mused. 'I'll see if I can find out where it's from. Did you get my message about this afternoon?'

'Oh, yes,' Janie said with feeling. 'I'll be there.'

Despite her enthusiasm, she was feeling extremely nervous when the time came. She'd changed into a sweatshirt and jeans (what *did* you wear to be hypnotised?) and put on a little lipstick in the hope it might cheer her up, but in fact nothing worked very well. She was fearful of what it would be like to be hypnotised. She was fearful of what ghastly memories would arise if it worked. And she was even more fearful of what would happen if it didn't. She supposed at that stage she'd have to start taking Toby's theory seriously. But that hardly bore thinking about. What did you do to stop a haunting?

Toby was there in his work suit – he'd obviously not had time to go home and change – and he gave her his best smile, which helped. Dr Walker was there, as was Dr Redmond, but there was something changed about the office. She looked around twice before she realised what it was: they'd moved in a black leather psychiatrist's couch.

'I suppose I have to lie on that?'

'I thought that was your great ambition,' Dr Redmond said, and grinned.

It defused some of her tension. She tried tentatively sitting on the couch and found it surprisingly comfortable, although the leather creaked a lot. She looked from one doctor to the other. 'I want you to explain to me exactly what's going to happen before we start.'

'We'd planned to do that anyway,' Dr Walker said. 'What's going to happen is that you'll lie down on the couch – or you can sit in the easy chair, if that's more comfortable. Although *we'd* prefer the couch, if it's all the same to you.' She waved her hand vaguely. 'But it really doesn't matter. Once you're comfortable, Dr Redmond will do his trick – he's the hypnotist of this little team.'

Janie turned to Redmond. 'How will you do your trick, Dr Redmond? Have you brought your watch?'

Redmond frowned. 'Watch?'

'Cartoon show called *Road Runner*,' Toby put in. 'Road Runner sometimes hypnotises Coyote by swinging a watch in front of him.' He mimed the action, then dropped his voice into a sinister growl. 'You are getting sleepy. Keep your eyes on the watch.'

'No watch,' said Dr Redmond. 'I simply talk to you, see if I can persuade you to relax.'

'What happens if it doesn't work?'

Redmond shrugged. 'Then it doesn't work.'

'Do you think it will?'

'Yes. You're already falling spontaneously into trance. Hypnotic induction should be a piece of cake. Unless you fight me, of course. I can do nothing unless you co-operate.'

That was sort of reassuring. She licked her dry lips. 'OK, suppose it *does* work, what happens? Is it like passing out?'

Dr Redmond shook his head. 'You don't lose consciousness at all. Most people think you do, but you don't. You'll start to feel very relaxed, then a little dreamy and eventually you'll be in a position where you can begin to remember whatever it is you've buried.'

'If I've buried anything.'

'Quite,' said Dr Redmond. His tone suggested he was fairly sure she'd buried something.

'Will I remember about it afterwards?'

'Yes,' Redmond said. 'If you're a deep-trance subject – and you may well be – there's a tendency to forget afterwards. They call it post-hypnotic amnesia. But it's easy enough to counteract – I simply give you a suggestion to remember.'

'All right,' Janie said, 'can this thing harm me?'

'If you mean being hypnotised,' Dr Redmond said, 'the answer is no. The only *physical* effect hypnosis has is to lower your heart rate and blood pressure a little, both of which are generally beneficial. Your muscles relax and your brain generates more alpha rhythms than usual and that's it. No physical harm at all.'

She was about to ask him another question when he surprised her by going on. 'But I have to tell you, I can't give you any guarantees about *emotional* damage. If you *have* buried something, it's because you *wanted* to bury it. I'll be as gentle as I can, but it may hurt a lot when it comes up again. Which brings me to another point. Toby's here because you wanted him here and Dr Walker thought it would be a good idea for you to have somebody familiar holding your hand, so to speak. I just want to remind you that the material we unearth may be of a very personal nature. So do you still want him here? I've talked to Toby about this and he'd completely understand if you'd prefer not.'

Janie looked at Toby and gave a small smile. 'I'd prefer Toby to stay.'

Dr Walker said, 'Is there anything else, Janie? Anything at all? Now's the time to ask.'

An earlier thought popped back into her head. 'Did you find my quotation? The thing about the pale horse.'

'Yes, as a matter of fact I did,' Dr Walker said. 'I almost forgot to tell you. It's from the Bible – the New Testament Book of Revelation. It's part of the prophecy about the end of the world. Rather appropriate I would have thought – something with no cure like the Black Death must have seemed the end of the world in the fourteenth century.'

'How about now?' Janie asked. 'Can we cure it now?'

'Oh, we can cure it now all right. Tetracycline

will do the trick. So will streptomycin or chloramphenicol. The only trouble is, you have to adminster the antibiotics very quickly. If you wait more than a few hours, your patient's just as dead as if they'd lived in the Middle Ages.'

Janie turned back to Dr Redmond. 'You said about Toby holding my hand. Would it be all right if he *really* held my hand.'

Dr Redmond smiled again. 'It would be *perfectly* all right,' he said.

Janie stretched on the couch and held out her hand to Toby. 'OK,' she said, 'let's do it!'

EIGHTEEN

They drew the curtains to dim the light. Toby
came across and took her hand. Dr Redmond
moved his chair behind the head of the couch.
Janie squeezed Toby's hand convulsively. She
was feeling far more nervous than she showed,
but beyond the nervousness there was a deeper,
multi-layered fear. Fear of what was about to
happen, fear of the unknown and most of all, fear
that the hypnotherapy would not work and she
would be left for ever with the nightmares and
the trances. She took a deep, sighing breath and
closed her eyes.

'No, keep your eyes open,' Dr Redmond
instructed softly. 'I'd like you to look up at the
ceiling and fix your eyes on the light fitting.'

'OK.' The way the couch was positioned, the
light fitting was a little behind her head so she
had to roll her eyes backwards to see it. The bulb
was surrounded by a hideous pink shade she
hadn't noticed before.

'That's perfect,' Dr Redmond said. 'Comfy?'

She wiggled her bottom a little and the couch
squeaked. 'Yes, I'm fine.'

'Good,' Redmond said. 'Now I want you to

keep your eyes fixed on the light, try to relax as much as possible, and in a moment, as I talk to you, you will find your eyes are beginning to tire and your eyelids are beginning to grow heavy.'

Her eyes certainly *were* getting tired, Janie thought, but it was nothing to do with being hypnotised. She really had to roll them all the way back to see that damn light fitting. It was about as uncomfortable an eye position as she could imagine. No wonder they were feeling tired.

'Growing so heavy,' Dr Redmond repeated, 'so very, very heavy.' He had a light voice, not at all the sinister deep velvet you'd imagine a hypnotist would need, but he had slowed his speech to a nice restful delivery. 'So very heavy that you just want to close them and you *can* close them. Close your eyes now, Janie, and simply rest and relax.'

She closed her eyes gratefully. It really had been an enormous strain keeping them fixed on that hideous pink shade.

'Just lie there in the darkness and allow your body to relax,' Dr Redmond told her softly. 'You're safe and well, easy and relaxed. Toby's here to look after you so you're completely safe, completely relaxed. You can let yourself relax even more deeply.'

Janie moved a little to relax more deeply and the leather of the couch creaked. That creaking was really irritating, she thought. There was no way she was going to be hypnotised if every time she moved the couch creaked. She wondered if she should mention it to Dr Redmond, get him to put her in the chair, but she decided against it for the moment. She didn't really want to move.

'So relaxed,' said Dr Redmond, 'that you don't really want to move. And growing more relaxed so that now you are beginning to feel heavy. Heavy like lead. As if every molecule and fibre of your body is turing to heavy, heavy lead.'

She felt her hand in Toby's hand and was glad he'd come. Toby was really rather special.

Her mind must have wandered, because she suddenly realised Dr Redmond was saying, '. . . away. Away from worries, away from cares, away from all responsibilities. Drifting, floating, to the sound of my voice . . .'

Janie sighed deeply.

She blinked. She was no longer lying on the couch. It was the weirdest thing she'd ever experienced. Weirder than the nightmares, weirder than the sudden shifts into another ghastly time. She was floating somewhere near the corner of the ceiling. Actually floating like some Transcendental Meditation guru practising his levitation!

Janie couldn't believe it. One minute she'd been lying on her back on the couch, holding Toby's hand and now she was floating just below the ceiling like some stupid balloon. Except she didn't *feel* like a stupid balloon. She felt perfectly normal in every respect, except one.

The hideous pink lampshade was less than a metre away from her nose. She could see a dead fly trapped in one of the frills. She could see the fraying of the flex and a small chip in the fitting where the flex entered the ceiling. She drifted and found she could actually read the wattage and the Mazda brand-name on the light bulb.

She looked down.

Dr Walker was perched on a corner of her desk over by the window. She was wearing a tweed skirt and a heavy blue shirt. One leg dangled, swinging to and fro. She was watching Dr Redmond intently.

Dr Redmond was seated behind the couch, leaning forward slightly, his hands clasped on his lap. '. . . and deeper,' he was saying, 'deeper still and deeper until you pass into a safe, warm sleep . . .'

There was a dark-haired girl lying on the couch, dressed in a white sweatshirt and tight blue jeans. To Janie's sudden annoyance, she noticed Toby was holding her hand. 'Hey!' she called.

'. . . deeper and deeper and deeper,' Dr Redmond droned. 'You are now more deeply . . .'

The girl on the couch was *her*! Janie stared down in total disbelief. Toby hadn't run off with some floozie – he was still holding *her* hand. It was as if she'd somehow floated up out of her body, leaving her body *behind*, until she was now floating just below the ceiling looking down at what was happening in the room.

Except that was impossible, not least of all because she still had her body with her. She was floating by the ceiling still wearing her jeans and sweatshirt, still as real and solid—

Janie reached out to touch the hideous pink lampshade. She reached out a real, solid hand on the end of a real solid arm. But that real solid hand went right through the lampshade, right through the electric light bulb.

'. . . and now,' murmured Dr Redmond, 'you no longer want to move at all . . .'

'Hey!' shouted Janie, suddenly delighted. 'I'm up here!'

No one looked up. No one paid any attention at all. It was as if they couldn't hear her. She was like a ghost. She was floating in the room like a ghost!

She wondered abruptly if she really *was* a ghost, if she'd died down there on the couch. The thought did not worry her at all. She didn't feel dead, not even slightly. And when she looked down at the Janie on the couch, she saw that Janie was still breathing.

The room, she noticed, was no longer gloomy, although the curtains were still drawn. It was bathed in a flat, bluish light, like moonlight, except perhaps a little brighter. She could not see the source. And there were other, subtle changes as well. There was a hat-stand by the door she hadn't noticed before; and a tall Chinese vase on Dr Walker's desk.

There was a brightness building in one corner.

'. . . deeper asleep than you have ever been before . . .' intoned Dr Redmond. The Janie on the couch moved a little and the leather creaked again.

The brightness in the corner became a nebulous,

123

misty form and then a definite shape. The Janie by the ceiling found she couldn't take her eyes off it.

'Now, Janie,' said Dr Redmond in a much brisker intonation, 'I want you to go back, back in your mind, to that day in Maris Caulfield . . .'

The brightness in the corner had taken on the form of a woman. Janie couldn't see her face, but there was something dreadfully familiar about the posture and the shape. Faintly, she could make out the outlines of a long skirt and an apron.

'. . . when you entered the plague house which had your name on the plaque and . . .'

This is dangerous, Janie thought suddenly. For the first time since she'd found herself outside her physical body, she began to feel afraid.

The shape in the corner had become a spirit form, a vaguely luminous figure like a special effect in a Dracula Gothic drama. Janie knew who she was even before her head turned and raised to look briefly in Janie's direction. It was the woman she'd seen in the bedroom at Maris. But more than that, it was the woman she'd *been* during her trance visions. It was Jayne Hyde, the tenant farmer's wife, who'd died like all the others in the great pestilence that struck the Caul Field in the fourteenth century.

Their eyes locked.

Janie felt fear exploding through her like nothing she had felt before. It was fear beyond her fear of the hunchback, or the dreadful bloated corpses she had seen. It was a humming dread that almost paralysed her being.

'No!' she whispered. Then, more loudly, 'No!'

'. . . and so, as you relax even more deeply . . .' murmured Dr Redmond's voice.

The luminous figure of Jayne Hyde glided from the corner of the room and slipped into the body of Janie Hyde lying on the couch.

NINETEEN

The scene below suddenly snapped into a crystal clarity that emphasised every detail.

The body of Janie Hyde on the couch convulsed abruptly, arching upwards at the hip to form a brief bow between head and heels before subsiding just as quickly. The hand Toby held was snatched away.

Dr Walker's foot stopped swinging and her jaw dropped. 'What—?'

'Relax deeply,' Dr Redmond ordered, his voice low and soothing, but with a sudden injection of urgency. 'You're fine, Janie. You're quite safe.'

Janie Hyde's body thrashed. Her head lashed from side to side.

'What's the matter with her, Doctor?' Toby asked urgently.

'Lie still, Janie,' Dr Redmond commanded. 'Relax more deeply. Sleep!'

Janie by the ceiling watched with fascinated horror. The body on the couch no longer looked like her own. Couldn't they see it? The face was undergoing a change, growing fuller and . . . well, *older*. It no longer looked like a girl's face. And her body seemed fuller too, as if it had begun to swell.

Dr Walker was at Dr Redmond's side. 'What's happening, Paul?'

But Dr Redmond had no time to answer. 'Easy, Janie, easy. You're quite safe. Nothing can harm you.'

But something *was* harming her. Something was contorting her face into a grimace. Something was convulsing her body into another arc. Something was flailing her arms. The lips writhed in the contorted face and guttural, growling sounds emerged.

Toby stood up so suddenly his chair tipped and crashed backwards on to the floor. He backed away from the couch in horror. 'Oh my God!' he exclaimed, his voice scarcely louder than a whisper.

'What's happening to her?' Dr Walker asked again, more urgently.

Dr Redmond shook his head. 'I don't know. I've never seen anything like this before.' He reached out to place a hand on the girl's forehead, but she slapped it away violently.

'Do something!' Toby shouted. He was staring at the body on the couch with the riveted attention of a hunting dog.

Dr Walker turned to him. 'I think it might be better if you left, Toby,' she said quietly. She placed a hand on his shoulder.

'I'm going nowhere!' Toby hissed. For a moment he looked as though he might strike her, but he only said, 'Something's gone wrong, hasn't it?'

'Yes,' Dr Walker said. She turned from Toby back to Dr Redmond.

'Janie,' Dr Redmond was saying urgently, 'listen to me, Janie.'

The body of Janie Hyde sat bolt upright and opened its eyes. It swung both feet on to the floor. The head turned towards Dr Redmond. There was a corpse-like blankness of expression that was hideous to see. The lips writhed again and the body croaked a single word.

'What did she say?' asked Dr Walker.

Dr Redmond shook his head.

'She said "Help"!' snapped Toby, who had been further away than either of them.

'We'll help you, Janie,' Dr Redmond said soothingly. 'Why don't you just lie back dow—'

But the creature inhabiting Janie Hyde's body did not lie back down. She looked directly at Redmond and said, quite clearly this time, 'They be dead. They be all dead, every one.'

Dr Redmond looked at his colleague, then back at the seated figure of the girl. He seemed totally at a loss.

Dr Walker leaned forward. 'Who's dead, Janie?'

'My kin. All dead.'

Frowning, Dr Walker said, 'Your father and your mother?'

'Oh aye.' Her voice was not Janie's voice. It was a richer contralto, burred with an accent that sounded a little like Dorset or Devon, yet like neither.

'But your parents are alive,' Dr Redmond put in.

Both women ignored him. 'Who else?' asked Dr Walker.

'My husband,' said the woman in Janie's body. A tear squeezed from her eye and rolled down her cheek.

'Husband?' Redmond echoed, bewildered.

'The priest's dead,' said the strange contralto voice. 'And the Squire and all in the Caul Field. Even the smith's boy died at the end.'

'This is a secondary personality!' Dr Redmond gasped. He turned excitedly to Dr Walker. 'She's exhibiting a secondary personality!'

'It's not a secondary personality!' Janie screamed down from the ceiling. 'Something's taken over my body!'

No one heard her. 'It's certainly not Janie,' Dr Walker murmured worriedly. She dropped her voice. 'You don't think she's tripped over into psychosis?'

Redmond said equally quietly, 'It may just be a bizarre reaction to hypnosis. Let's hope so for her sake.'

'Wake her up!' Toby screamed. 'I don't want her like this!'

'Perhaps we'd better,' Dr Walker murmured.

'When I snap my fingers,' Dr Redmond said firmly, 'you will awaken fully and return to your normal consciousness.'

'Be you the Sheriff's man?' asked Janie suddenly.

Dr Redmond snapped his fingers. 'Wake up, Janie!'

The girl on the couch lurched forward and spat violently in his face. 'Bastard!' she said. 'All are dead because of you!'

Dr Redmond jerked his head back, stunned. Toby suddenly shouted, 'That's not Janie! For God's sake, that's not Janie!' His voice was high with panic.

From her perspective by the ceiling, Janie Hyde knew he was right. Something was inside her body, using it like a puppet. And her body was beginning to take on the shape of the inhabiting soul. Her breasts looked heavier. There was a roll of fat around her stomach. Her face had changed out of all recognition. Why was Toby the only one to see this?

The creature on the couch flung itself violently on Dr Redmond, hands curled into talons, fingernails raking for his eyes. 'I'll kill you, Fitz-Gerald!' it screamed.

But Dr Redmond moved faster than Janie would have believed possible. He slid from his chair, ducked beneath the raking hands, and grabbed the creature's wrists. 'Help me, Janice!' he called to Dr Walker. 'We need to restrain her.'

Dr Walker grabbed one wrist and together they tried to wrestle the creature back on to the couch. Janie watched in horror as her body kicked and twisted with mind-numbing fury. At one point her teeth fastened on Dr Redmond's hand so that blood spurted and spattered his face. For a moment it seemed even the combined strength of the two adults would not be enough, but then Toby ran forward and grabbed her legs.

The three of them somehow forced her back and pressed down on her.

Suddenly the fight was over. Janie's body went limp, but her breath rasped and her chest heaved as if she was having trouble breathing. 'They did not bury me in consecrated ground,' she gasped.

Cautiously, Dr Redmond and the others relaxed their grip.

'Who did not bury you in consecrated ground?' Dr Walker asked gently.

'Fitz—' The breathing was growing more laboured. 'FitzGerald. Sheriff FitzGerald, God's curse upon him, may he rot in Hell.'

'Gently,' murmured Dr Redmond as if hypnotic suggestion might suddenly begin to take effect.

'Help . . .' gasped the creature on the couch. 'Must help . . . me . . .' She was gulping for breath as a drowning man gulps for air.

'You must try to rest now, dear,' Dr Walker said. 'You've had a bad exper—'

'Must bury me in consecrated ground, else . . . else how shall I have hope . . .' she was wheezing like an old, old man, '. . . hope of resurrection.'

'She's having an asthma attack!' said Toby suddenly.

'My God, the asthma!' exclaimed Dr Walker, shock on her face. 'I completely forgot.'

Dr Redmond said, 'I'm sorry – I forgot too. Her attacks are fairly rare.'

Dr Walker spun round to Toby. 'Does she take medication?'

'She has an inhaler,' Toby said.

On the couch, Janie's body began a strenuous whooping wheeze and convulsed again. Her eyes bulged and her lips took on a distinctly bluish tinge.

'Where does she keep it?' Walker asked urgently.

Toby was watching what was happening on the couch, his eyes wide. 'In her bag.' He dragged his gaze away and looked at Dr Walker. 'But she didn't have her bag with her when she came in.'

Dr Redmond said bleakly, 'She must have left it in her room!'

Dr Walker ran to her desk and slammed a button on the intercom. 'Sandra,' she said, 'this is an emergency. Anti-asthma medication in here. Fast.'

On the couch, the wheeze turned into a regular, dragged-out moan, like an animal in the final throes of an agonising death. Janie's body began to jerk spasmodically, small movements that were somehow far more terrifying than the larger, more dramatic convulsions.

'Christ!' exclaimed Dr Redmond. 'She's going into cardiac arrest!'

By the desk, Dr Walker slammed the intercom button again. 'Cardiac emergency!' she snapped.

By the ceiling, Janie's paralysis broke. The thing had taken possession of her body! And unless she did something fast, her body would die! She flew downwards like an arrow – and in her panic scarcely even noticed that she *flew* – and embraced the twitching, jerking body on the couch. An instinct too deep to question told her she had to blend with that body, had to inhabit that body, had to take control of that body before it was destroyed.

It was like slamming into a brick wall.

She knew what was happening (without knowing how she knew). Her body, her own body that had grown with her for all these years, was already occupied. Another soul was living in it. Another entity had *taken possession*.

And that other soul had to be evicted!

Janie plunged again. She could feel the energy of the other entity, the chilling, draining touch of the ghost. It was as if they locked together like wrestlers, then Janie felt pain of a type she had never experienced before, an immense cold burn that ran from the top of her head to the tip of her toes. And with that pain came another, a pressure on her chest like the grip of some unimaginable vice.

'Get out!' Janie screamed at the ghost. 'Get out of my body!'

She seemed to slip sideways. Suddenly she was in another space. The world around her was twitching and jerking, a world without air, a world of crushing pain. She could see the woman she'd seen in the bedroom at Maris, and the woman was smiling a triumphant smile. Then the pain became a flood of blood and everything went black.

TWENTY

She swam slowly to consciousness in what was almost, but not quite, a darkened room. She was in a bed, in unfamiliar pyjamas, and her chest felt as if it had been through a mangle. For a moment she was so exhausted she could only lie and stare upwards into the gloom. The asthma attack was finished. Her breathing was unlaboured and clear. She listened to it for a moment, enjoying the sensation of cool, clean air entering her lungs without obstruction. But her heightened senses picked up the sound of other breathing to her left.

There was someone with her in the room!

Panic drove the tiredness from her instantly and she sat bolt upright.

'Hey, easy!' came Toby's voice. 'It's only me!'

She turned and found him sitting fully-dressed in a chair by her bedside. He gave her a cautious smile.

Janie sank back on to her pillows. 'What happened?' she asked. 'Where am I?'

'Still at the clinic,' Toby said. 'They put you in here because of the gear.'

She followed the direction of his gaze. The far

side of the room was jammed with medical equipment. She suddenly realised there was a heart monitor on her chest. A blip was bouncing across a small green screen on one of the machines, but it did not beep the way this sort of equipment did in the movies.

'I've just been made an honorary nurse,' Toby grinned. 'I volunteered to keep you under observation.' He held up a button on a long flex. 'If I press this, seventy-eight emergency teams come crashing in and we're at war with China.'

'Wow,' Janie said. 'That bad?'

The grin faded. 'Bad enough, sweetheart,' he said in Humphrey Bogart's voice. 'Can you remember any of it?'

'I remember something taking over my body,' Janie said. Maybe *that* would be enough to convince him she was going loopy, but she didn't care.

Toby nodded. 'That's what I figured.'

'You did?'

'It was fairly obvious if you weren't locked into the idea that ghosts are tape recordings,' Toby said sourly. 'How are you feeling?'

She considered for a moment. Oddly enough, she wasn't feeling all that bad. Even the pain in her chest was fading. 'I think I'll live,' she said.

'Good,' said Toby. 'Because we have to get out of here.'

Janie blinked. 'Sorry?'

Toby leaned forward earnestly. 'It was the woman in Maris Caulfield, wasn't it? The one with your name?'

Janie nodded.

'She'd been dead for more than six hundred years.'

'I know.'

'And she tried to take over your body.'

'Didn't just try,' Janie said. 'It nearly killed me getting her out.'

'Next time it might *really* kill you,' Toby said. 'Unless we make sure there *isn't* any next time.'

Janie stared at him for a long moment, then asked, 'How?'

'The Jayne Hyde who lived in Maris at the time of the Black Death was one of the last to catch the disease,' Toby said. 'By the time she died, there was nobody left to bury her. Sheriff FitzGerald eventually sent his men in, but the corpses were just dumped into holes dug more or less where they lay. They weren't buried in consecrated ground.'

'There was no room in the churchyard,' Janie murmured.

'Jayne Hyde was a very religious woman,' Toby said. 'She believed if you weren't buried in consecrated ground, you had no chance of resurrection.' He looked at her soberly. 'She still does.'

Janie didn't know how he knew all this – maybe he'd been talking to the Maris rector again – but she did know, with absolute certainty, he was right. Jayne Hyde, who died of the most hideous disease ever visited on the Middle Ages, still wanted to be buried in consecrated ground.

This was the reason she'd been haunting. This was the reason she'd been sending Janie visions and nightmares.

'Why me?' Janie asked tiredly.

Toby spread his hands. 'You've the same name. Maybe you're related. Maybe she's a distant ancestor. Maybe you're susceptible. Maybe you were just in the wrong place at the wrong time. It doesn't matter. What matters is putting a stop to the haunting.'

'I don't know how!' snapped Janie desperately.

'That's simple,' Toby said. 'We have to bury her in consecrated ground.' He stood up. 'Get dressed. I don't think we have time to waste.'

'You mean go *tonight*?'

'You think they're going to let you out of here this side of Christmas after what happened?' Toby said. 'They're going to run tests and call specialists and shrink your head to the size of a pin. You nearly bought it back there – you know that. They're going to want to find out why and guard their asses about whose fault it was. Meanwhile our friend from Maris Caulfield is lurking wherever ghosts lurk waiting for a second chance to get her hands on your sweet little bod. If we're going to do anything about this mess, I reckon we have to do it tonight, while they think you're still sleeping, recovering from your dreadful ordeal and I'm the only one watching you.'

'But we don't even know where Jayne Hyde was *buried*!' Janie protested.

'Yes, we do,' Toby said. 'At least I think we

do. The rector told me there was an old plague burial at the back of her house – the one you broke into. Chances are that's her.'

What he was actually suggesting suddenly dawned on Janie. 'You mean we go and *dig her up*?'

'That's right.'

'In the middle of the night?'

'When else?'

'And then we dig a fresh grave in the local churchyard and put the body in that?' She had a vivid mental picture of the Maris constable stumbling on them as they dragged the corpse towards the open grave. *'Allo, 'allo, 'allo*, he would say, *what's going on here?*

'There won't be a body after all this time,' Toby said. 'They buried plague victims in lime where they could. I expect all we'll be dealing with is a few bones, maybe a skull. We won't even have to dig a deep grave in the churchyard – just a hole big enough to take them. The important thing is that it's consecrated ground.'

Janie stared at him in astonishment. He'd actually worked all this out. He actually planned to do it. *And he's right*, a small voice whispered in her mind. *It's like a horror movie, but it's the only way you have a chance to lay the ghost.* She suspected he was right about the timing too. She'd had convulsions, asthma, what looked like a heart attack and the emergence of a 'secondary personality'. It was touch and go whether they would ever let her out of hospital again. 'But we've no way of getting there,' she pleaded feebly. She had an idea he might have worked that out as well.

'We get there by car,' Toby said. 'It isn't far.'

'You can't drive!'

'Yes, I can,' he told her. 'I just haven't passed my test.'

'But you haven't got a car!'

'That's true, but I know where we can borrow one.'

'At this hour of the night?' Janie hissed.

Toby sighed. 'Dr Redmond's Jag is in the car park outside.'

Janie blinked. She wouldn't have believed it, but an experience that started with a ghost was steadily getting even more fantastic. 'Dr Redmond is going to lend you his *Jag*?'

Toby refused to meet her eyes. 'I'm sure he'd be happy to if we asked him.'

'But you're not going to ask him.'

'I can't find him,' said Toby, deadpan.

This was unbelievable. Her boyfriend whom she thought she *knew* was calmly talking about 'borrowing' a car without the owner's permission, driving without a licence to Maris Caulfield, digging up an ancient grave then re-burying the bones in the local churchyard – all in the middle of the night! 'How are you going to start it?' she asked.

Toby muttered something inaudible.

'What?'

'Hot-wire it,' Toby said.

'You can *hot-wire* a car?'

'It's easy.' He changed the subject suddenly.

139

'Listen, none of this is the point. The point is unless we do something and do it fast, you're going to be in big trouble. Now, will you get some clothes on and let's get *moving*!'

I must be mad, Janie thought as she slid out of bed and started to pull on a sweater and jeans over her pyjamas.

TWENTY-ONE

If she'd thought herself mad while creeping out of the clinic, Janie was doubly sure of it now, standing in the yard of a haunted house by moonlight, planning to dig up an ancient plague pit and transfer any bones she found to the local churchyard.

'This is the house?' Toby asked. He'd hot-wired the Jaguar like a professional, then driven it, sedate as a little old lady, to Maris. She'd been absolutely certain they would be stopped, but they weren't.

She nodded. 'Yes.'

'Spooky place, isn't it?'

It was actually even more spooky than she remembered, but there was one thing to be thankful for – the moonlight wasn't quite bright enough to let her read her own name on the plaque. 'Can't we get this over with?' she asked. In the same way she'd been certain they would be stopped, she was now certain someone would happen along the lane. The sleek shape of Dr Redmond's Jag – Dr Redmond's *stolen* Jag – was parked on the verge. They were somewhere they had absolutely no right to be. And if they told the truth, they were about to engage on a little grave-robbing before they went off to desecrate a churchyard.

Is there room in the churchyard? a small voice asked in her mind. But she already knew there would be room. The churchyard had been greatly extended since Jayne Hyde pushed the corpses of her parents into the yawning grave.

'Hurry up!' she snapped at Toby. She looked around. Where to dig? The grounds behind the house weren't exactly a country estate, but they were big enough. And besides, the boundaries weren't the same now as they were in the four-teenth century – she remembered that from her visions. The pit that contained Jayne Hyde's bones could be almost anywhere. More to the point, she realised abruptly, they hadn't brought spades. It was all too nerve-racking and disorgan-ised. 'We didn't bring any spades,' she added, voicing the thought.

'Shit!' hissed Toby. 'I knew there was something!'

Maybe they should just leave. Maybe there was some other way of laying the ghost. Some-thing moved in the bushes to her right and she almost jumped out of her skin. 'What's that?'

'Owl taking a mouse, I think,' said Toby. He seemed to have nerves like hawsers. He caught her arm. 'Hey, what's that?'

She could see his finger pointing to the spot where the builder's heavy machinery was silhou-etted against the skyline like a giant insect. 'It's a JCB,' she told him. 'It doesn't look as if it's been moved since the last time I was here.'

'Then we don't need spades,' said Toby cheerfully.

Janie's nerve broke completely. She grabbed his arm. 'You can't!' she said. 'Those things make enough noise to wake the—' She stopped, realising what she'd been about to say. 'Come on, Toby, you'll have half the village down on us!'

'No, I won't,' Toby said. 'Sure it makes a noise, but people aren't that curious. They'll just assume it's workmen.'

'In the middle of the night?'

'They often run machinery at night. Road-building. That sort of thing. So it doesn't interfere with traffic.'

This isn't road building! she wanted to scream at him. But even by moonlight she could see that look on his face, the one that crept into place when he decided to be stubborn.

'Can you *work* something like that?' she asked. 'Can you even *start* something like that?'

'Watch me,' Toby said.

He scampered up the side of the machine like a monkey and disappeared into the cab. Watching him, Janie noted the cab door was unlocked and wondered if all heavy machinery was left like that. She supposed it was unlikely to be taken by joyriders.

There was a moment that stretched to eternity as she stood nervously in the darkness. Then the JCB engine coughed once and roared into life. Despite herself, Janie jumped. She was certain someone would come.

Light suddenly flooded the site as Toby found

the headlights. Her stomach knotted as the machine lurched, then rumbled forward on its caterpillar treads.

To her surprise, he could obviously control the thing very well – at least he didn't knock anything down. He positioned it between the building and the orchard, brought the scoop down slowly, then climbed down from the cab leaving the engine running and the lights on. 'Piece of cake,' he remarked. He pushed past her and headed for the car.

He came back carrying a shallow cardboard box. 'Better get equipped,' he said, pushing it towards her.

Janie looked into the box. It contained a selection of surgical masks and gloves. She looked up at Toby, his face stark in the glare of the headlights. 'What's this and where did you get it?' She knew the answer to the second part without being told. He'd taken the gloves and masks from the clinic. It was small potatoes after you'd stolen a car and a JCB.

'From the clinic,' Toby confirmed. 'We need to get kitted up before we start digging.'

'In surgeon's gear?' Janie asked, bewildered. For an instant it crossed her mind that she was hallucinating again, that this whole lunatic escapade was going on purely in her mind.

'The plague bacillus is anaerobic,' Toby said.

She frowned at him. 'What's anaerobic?'

'Doesn't need air,' Toby said.

For a moment she stared at him, stunned. He couldn't be saying what she thought he was saying. It was too incredible to be true and if it *was* true then what they were planning was insane. 'You don't mean the bacillus is still *active* down there?'

'It may be,' Toby said calmly.

'After *six hundred years*?'

'I know it doesn't sound very likely,' Toby said, 'and the truth is nobody knows for sure, but the Government takes it very seriously. They won't allow excavation of any plague burial grounds anywhere in the country.'

'You mean we're breaking the law digging here?' As if they hadn't been breaking the law trespassing, using a JCB, damaging private property and God only knew what else.

'Look,' said Toby patiently, 'it's probably not active at all. There's no real evidence. The Government is just . . . taking sensible precautions. Which is what we're doing with the masks and gloves.'

Janie felt her stomach turn into a tight, hard ball. She *remembered* what the plague bacillus could do. She remembered the blackened, bloated bodies, the angry swellings oozing pus, the cracked blue lips, the staring, hopeless eyes. Most of all she remembered how terrifyingly quickly the disease struck. Jayne Hyde's husband Alan had been well in the morning and dead in the afternoon. Dr Walker said that even now, even with modern drugs, you had to administer the antibiotics within hours or your patient was dead. And the pestilence spread like wildfire.

'Toby, we *can't* open up an old plague pit –

it's too dangerous!' How could he even *dream* of doing it?

But Toby set the box down and reached out to take her by both shoulders. 'You know I love you, don't you?'

It stopped her short. He'd never actually said it before. 'I—' she said. Her mouth moved, but no further words would come out.

'You're being *haunted*,' he told her. 'The doctors may think it's some sort of psychological bullshit, but we know better. I've watched you these last few weeks and you've been going through hell. You can't sleep, you fall down stairs, you're stuck in a psychiatric clinic and just a few hours ago this thing nearly killed you. Janie, we have to get you out from under this thing. We *have* to lay the ghost. And if that means opening up a plague pit, that's what we'll do.' He released her shoulders. 'We'll put on masks and gloves before we handle anything that comes out of the pit – *anything*.' He looked deep into her eyes. 'We'll be fine.'

And at that moment Janie felt he was right. They *would* be fine. They would find Jayne Hyde's bones and take them to the churchyard and they would be fine. The haunting would stop. The nightmare would cease. She would be fine. 'I love you too, Toby,' she said.

Together they pulled on the rubber gloves and tied the surgical masks around their mouth and nose. 'Watch out for bones,' Toby told her, his voice muffled by the mask. 'I don't have such a detailed view up there.' Then he was climbing back into the cab of the JCB. The engine roared violently, there was a metallic clanking and the great arm plunged the digger bucket into the earth.

Janie watched it like one in a dream. The topsoil disappeared like magic as Toby created a huge trench that ran almost up to the back door of the house. With only a rough idea of where the remains were buried, he had obviously determined to cover as much of an area as possible.

The noise and movement were hypnotic. The lights of the JCB cut swathes through the darkness. Toby handled the machine as if he'd been trained to use it – although she supposed it was probably easy enough to dig a simple pit in the open once you had the hang of the controls.

She almost missed it. The metal teeth of the bucket plunged, hesitated, lifted and swung to deposit clay on the growing heap to the right, then swung back again and started another descent. Directly below it was a human head.

'Stop!' Janie screamed. She doubted he could have heard her over the racket of the digger, but he caught her wildly waving arms. The bucket arm jerked once, then froze. Toby cut the engine.

The sudden silence was like a body blow. Janie stared, fascinated, at the head. It was a hideous object. Some freak of chemical composition in the soil had mummified a portion of the face. But other portions had been eaten away to the bone, giving it a nightmare grimace. The eye sockets, long empty of eyes, seemed to gaze directly at her. She knew, beyond argument or doubt, she was looking at the mortal remains of Jayne Hyde.

Toby was beside her. 'Is it her?'

Janie nodded. 'Yes.'

It didn't seem to occur to him to wonder how she knew. He moved forward without hesitation.

Janie shuddered. 'Careful.'

'Mask and gloves,' Toby said. 'We'll burn them later. We'll be fine.' Delicately he began to scrape the earth away with his gloved hands. In minutes he had freed the skull and what looked like a portion of a ribcage. 'This seems to be all there is,' he said. 'The lime must have eaten away the rest.'

A sudden, horrifying thought struck Janie. 'It's not affecting your gloves?'

'No, we're safe.' He lifted the skull with enormous reverence, using both hands, and stared directly into the hollow sockets of the eyes. 'Ghastly thing,' he murmured. He turned and passed it carefully to Janie. He turned back for the ribcage.

A torch shone in her face. 'What the hell do you think you're doing?' asked a rough male voice. 'Over here, lads – there's two of them!'

The JCB headlights were still on and she saw the uniforms as they stepped out of the darkness.

'Looks like they've been burying a body,' remarked one constable.

'Or digging one up.'

The policeman closest to her set down his torch. 'I'll have that, Miss,' he said firmly, reaching for the skull.

Janie watched in slow motion as his gloveless hands closed on the head. Out of the corner of her eye, she could see a second policeman plunge forward to snatch the ribcage from Toby's hands. Others were following him into the pit. None of them wore masks or gloves.

'No!' Janie screamed.

And once she began screaming she found she could not stop.

Authorities deny deaths due to Plague

Health Authorities continue to insist that the mystery illness which has spread through the North Devon village of Maris Caulfield has no connection with the bubonic plague which wiped out the entire village in the fourteenth century.

The illness, which has so far claimed the lives of eight victims – all but one of them members of the North Devon Constabulary – continues to spread despite strict quarantine restrictions on travel into or out of the area.

Despite the official position, intense speculation continues that the illness is, in fact, a form of bubonic plague.

Bubonic plague is an acute infection caused by the bacterium *Yersinia pestis*.

The first signs of illness appear suddenly. In a few hours the body temperature rises to about 40 deg C (104 deg F), and the victim becomes gravely ill, experiencing vomiting, muscular pain, mental disorientation, and delirium.

The lymph nodes throughout the body, especially those in the groin and the thighs, become enlarged and extremely painful.

The inflamed lymph nodes, called

buboes (from which the disease gets its name) become filled with pus, and the disease spreads through the body by way of the infected bloodstream and the lymphatic system.

In 60–90 per cent of untreated cases the infection is overwhelming and causes death within a few days.

A bubonic plague epidemic in the fourteenth century – known as the Black Death – killed 75 million people, about half the population of Europe.

Continued on page 5

EVENING STANDARD, THURSDAY, AUGUST 31.

Keith Gray

HUNTING THE CAT

It was huge; as long as a man is tall. Pale like a ghost it leapt from its den. . . Its face was twisted and savage, purely feral, its ears flat to its head. Its teeth and claws were already bloody.

Joseph and his father go away on a weekend's fishing trip, but their plans change when they find that there may be a big cat on the moors. It seems like a big adventure – until they discover the cat's den and the adventure turns into a nightmare.

"horribly scary before a wholly satisfying resolution."

Bookseller

Mary Downing Hahn

WAIT TILL HELEN COMES

He scraped away the dirt and moss to reveal the inscription. "'H.E.H. March 7, 1879-August 8, 1886. May she rest in peace.'"

'It's my initials,' Heather said suddenly. 'Heather Elizabeth Hill.' She touched the stone lightly. 'My age, too,' she added.

When Molly and Michael's mother and her new husband move to a house in the country, they have to get used to a different way of life – and to Heather, their whiny, unhappy step-sister. It's easy to dislike Heather but when Molly finds her alone in the woods, apparently talking to someone, she begins to get worried. What is the strange attraction for Heather of the unnamed gravestone? Why is it set apart from the others? As echoes of the past blend with the family tensions of the present, Molly realises that she must save Heather from the impending tragedy.

Frances Usher

FACE TO FACE

Someone was laughing and calling me. I didn't hear the words, just the voice, but I knew I was the one being called. Someone was calling and teasing and laughing. Where? Behind me? . . . No, in front. Or was it only in my head?

Nick's dreams are driving him mad – running down endless corridors where he is haunted by the laughter of a girl with dark hair. Are the dreams a warning that destiny will bring him together with the unknown girl in a terrible way? And then Nick sees the girl on a school bus . . .